THE OFFICIAL TRUCK HANDBOOK

FOR TRUCK DRIVERS

This handbook is only a guide. For official purposes, please refer to the Ontario Highway Traffic Act and regulations, the Truck Transportation Act and regulations, the Dangerous Goods Act and Federal Motor Vehicle Transport Act.

Professional drivers in Ontario can promote road safety by driving with skill and consideration for others.

Disponible en français
Demandez le «Guide officiel des camions»

Driving is a privilege — not a right

Introduction

This handbook is designed to help people applying for a class A or D driver's licence. It contains the information you need to meet the standards for those licences, and sets out the skills you will be expected to perform during a driving test.

In addition to the rules of the road, truck drivers need to have special operating skills and know the laws governing trucks. They are also expected to demonstrate safe driving practices.

The Ministry of Transportation (MTO) is committed to making Ontario's roads safer. In order to achieve this, the ministry has introduced many safety initiatives. In addition, more information pertaining to the laws governing the operators and drivers of commercial motor vehicles is being provided.

Ensuring the safety of all road users goes beyond drivers just having the ability to drive the vehicle safely. To drive a commercial motor vehicle, a wide range of skills and knowledge relating to vehicle maintenance, brakes, wheels and various laws is required.

Contents

GETTING YOUR LICENCE

I. Legislation

These Acts and regulations govern truck driving in Ontario.

1. The Highway Traffic Act (HTA) and regulations govern the driver, the vehicle and equipment, weight and size of loads, and the hours of service that a truck driver can operate.

2. The Dangerous Goods Act regulates the transportation of dangerous goods, including required documentation, handling, safety markings (labels and placards) and the certification of drivers.

3. The Truck Transportation Act governs the licensing of for hire carriers.

4. The Motor Vehicle Transport Act (Federal) regulates the for hire transportation of goods and people.

Transporting Dangerous Goods

There are nine classes of dangerous goods ranging from corrosives to flammable liquids, to environmentally hazardous materials. Drivers transporting dangerous goods must receive training from their current employer. The employer determines the level of training and once training is complete drivers are issued certificates from their current employer that they must carry when transporting dangerous goods.

II. Definitions

Commercial motor vehicle: any motor vehicle with a permanently attached truck or delivery body, including ambulances, hearses, casket wagons, fire apparatus, buses and tractors used for hauling purposes on highways.

Gross weight: the combined weight of vehicle and load.

Registered gross weight: the weight for which a permit has been issued under the HTA, the fee for which is based upon the weight of the vehicle or combination of vehicles and load.

Manufacturers' gross vehicle weight rating (MGVWR): the gross weight as specified by the manufacturer often attached as a decal or plate on the cab of a vehicle.

Motor vehicle: an automobile, motor-cycle, motor-assisted bicycle, unless otherwise indicated in the HTA, and any other vehicle propelled or driven other than by muscular power. Not included are the cars of electric or steam railways or other motor vehicles running only upon rails, or motorized snow vehicles, traction engines, farm tractors, or road-building machines.

Semi-trailer: a trailer designed to be operated with the forward part of its body or chassis resting upon the body or chassis of a towing vehicle.

Trailer: a vehicle drawn by a motor vehicle, but not a farm implement, a mobile home, another motor vehicle or any device not designed to transport persons or property, temporarily drawn, propelled or moved on a highway, and not a side car attached to a motorcycle. A trailer is considered a separate vehicle and not part of the motor vehicle by which it is drawn.

Vehicle: a motor vehicle, trailer, traction engine, farm tractor, road building machine or any vehicle drawn, propelled or driven by any kind of power, including muscular power, but does not include a motorized snow vehicle or the cars of electric or steam railways running only upon rails.

Self-propelled implement of husbandry: a self-propelled vehicle used specifically in farming — a farm tractor.

III. A and D licence classes and requirements

The quick check chart on pages 10 to 11 shows you what class of licence you need to drive different vehicles. A licensed driver wishing to learn to operate a truck or tractor trailer must be accompanied by a driver who holds a valid class D or class A licence respectively. Your driving competence will be assessed in a road test with a ministry examiner, an authorized employer, a community college. An authorized employer or community college known as a Recognized Authority may issue a certificate of driving competence for classes A, B, C, D, E, F and M.

Class A is authority for the operation of: a motor vehicle and towed vehicles where the towed vehicles exceed a total gross weight of 4600 kg (10,000 lbs.), or the operation of vehicles included in classes "D" and "G", but not buses carrying passengers, nor motorcycles.

Class D is authority for the operation of: any motor vehicle exceeding 11,000 kg (24,000 lbs.) gross weight or registered gross weight, and any combination of a motor vehicle exceeding a total gross weight or registered gross weight of 11,000 kg (24,000 lbs.), and towed vehicles not exceeding a total gross weight of 4600 kg (10,000 lbs.). It also allows you to operate vehicles included in class G, **but not a bus carrying passengers,** and not a motorcycle.

Minimum requirements for application:

An applicant for a class "A" or "D" driver's licence must:

- be at least 18 years of age
- hold a valid Ontario class "G" or higher licence or equivalent
- pass a test of operating knowledge of large trucks and tractor trailers
- meet vision standards
- provide a satisfactory medical certificate on application and periodically thereafter
- demonstrate driving competence during a road test in a combination of a motor vehicle exceeding 11,000 kg (24,000 lbs.) gross weight or registered gross weight and a towed vehicle exceeding 4600 kg (10,000 lbs.) total gross weight

All classes of driver licences authorize the operation of a motor-assisted bicycle (moped) and motorized snow vehicle.

Quick check chart

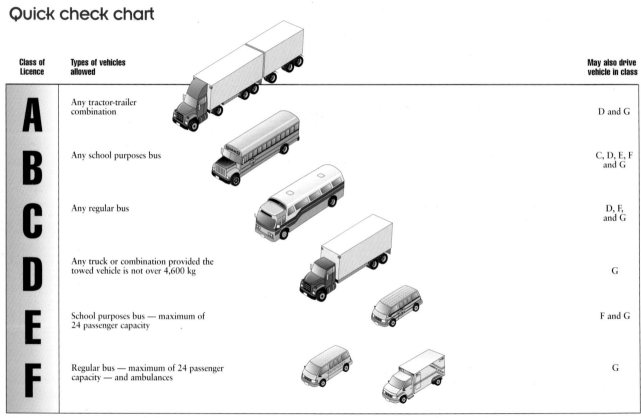

Class of Licence	Types of vehicles allowed	May also drive vehicle in class
A	Any tractor-trailer combination	D and G
B	Any school purposes bus	C, D, E, F and G
C	Any regular bus	D, F, and G
D	Any truck or combination provided the towed vehicle is not over 4,600 kg	G
E	School purposes bus — maximum of 24 passenger capacity	F and G
F	Regular bus — maximum of 24 passenger capacity — and ambulances	G

Diagram 1-1a

II. sub chapter

Class of Licence	Types of vehicles allowed	
G	Any car, van or small truck or combination of vehicle and towed vehicle up to 11,000 kg provided the towed vehicle is not over 4,600 kg.	
G1	Level One of graduated licensing Holders may drive Class G vehicles when accompanied by a fully licensed driver with at least four years of driving experience. Additional conditions apply.	
G2	Level Two of graduated licensing Holders may drive Class G vehicles without accompanying driver but are subject to certain conditions.	
M	Motorcycles Holders may also drive a Class G vehicle under the conditions that apply to a Class G1 licence holder.	
M1	Level One of graduated licensing Holders may drive a motorcycle under certain conditions.	
M2	Level Two of graduated licensing Holders may drive a motorcycle but only with a zero blood alcohol level. Holders may also drive a Class G vehicle under the conditions that apply to a Class G1 licence holder.	

Diagram 1-1b   A "Z" air brake endorsement is required on a driver's licence to operate any air brake equipped motor vehicles.

III. A and D licence classes and requirements

Higher classes

When applying for a class A or D licence, you must provide a completed satisfactory ministry medical certificate. Blank medical forms can be obtained from any Driver Examination Centre in Ontario. A licence will be refused if your physical or medical condition does not meet the standards outlined in the regulations of the Highway Traffic Act.

If your licence is conditional on wearing corrective lenses, do not drive without wearing them. Your medical practitioner or optometrist is required by law to report to the licensing authorities any physical, neurological, cardiovascular or other medical condition that might affect your safe operation of a motor vehicle.

People applying for a licence are required to provide the proper type of vehicle for the test.

You **should** study the operating manual for the vehicle to be used for the road test.

Road test

On the road test —

- You will be required to demonstrate a daily trip inspection commonly known as a circle check. (See pages 20 to 23). You will be required to name the item of equipment checked, and briefly describe its condition.
- Class A applicants may be required to uncouple and couple the units of the combination vehicle, or explain the procedures to the examiner.
- You will be required to drive in traffic and handle the vehicle safely.
- You may be required to reverse the vehicle into a parking bay or marked area.

Commercial Vehicle Operator Registration (CVOR) and vehicle documentation

The Commercial Vehicle Operator's Registration (CVOR) system is one method of monitoring the performance of commercial vehicle operators. An operator is the person responsible for the operation of a commercial motor vehicle including the conduct of the driver and the carriage of goods or passengers.

Under CVOR, operators of buses with a seating capacity of 10 or more and commercial motor vehicles with a registered or actual gross weight of over 4500 kg must obtain a CVOR certificate. Operators may obtain a CVOR certificate by submitting a CVOR application to the Ministry of Transportation. There is no charge for the initial registration.

Operators of emergency vehicles (ambulances, fire trucks), hearses, motor homes, buses used for personal transportation, vehicles leased for less than 30 days for personal use and empty vehicles while using dealer plates or in-transit permits are not required to obtain a CVOR certificate.

Upon issuance, the CVOR certificate reflects a unique nine-digit CVOR number. In addition to proof of insurance and vehicle registration, a legible copy of the certificate must be carried in the applicable vehicles at all times and be presented to police and MTO enforcement personnel on request. The original should be kept in a safe place since there is a replacement fee if it is lost, stolen or destroyed.

The CVOR record contains information that includes all convictions associated with the operator/carrier regardless of the person charged, all reportable collisions, detentions, and defaulted fines. Some examples are speeding, overweight, safety defects, or failing to produce a CVOR certificate. All items remain on the operator's record for five years from the date of the conviction.

III. A and D licence classes and requirements

If an operator's record becomes unacceptable, based on the fleet size and the number of items on the CVOR record, the operator may be sent a warning letter or asked to attend a meeting to discuss the record. If the operator's record does not improve, sanctions may be imposed. These include the cancellation/suspension of the CVOR certificate or the limitation of fleet size through the use of fleet limitation certificates.

Size and weight limits for commercial motor vehicles

Commercial motor vehicles are restricted in width to a limit of 2.6 m (8.53 ft). Exceptions are made for specialized equipment such as traction engines, threshing machines, snow removal equipment, and so on. Mirrors are not included when determining the width of a commercial vehicle.

Semi-trailers are limited to a length of 14.65 m (48 ft) or 16.15 m (53 ft) if the trailer and tractor meets special requirements.

No combination of vehicles is permitted to exceed a length of 23 m (74.75 ft) except double trailer combinations which meet special requirements for both trailers and the tractor.

All vehicles including their loads are limited to a height of 4.15 m (13.6 ft).

No vehicle or combination of vehicles is permitted to be operated on a highway when its gross weight exceeds the maximum weight permitted under Part VII of the Highway Traffic Act and its regulations.

To determine the gross allowable weight of a commercial vehicle several factors must be considered. Some of these include the number of axles, the size of the tires, the type of suspension, the distance between the axles, the type of load carried (aggregate or non-aggregate load) and the weight allowed on the steering axle.

Several formulas are used to determine the maximum allowable gross weight. These include calculating the sum of the weights allowed on each axle, the registered gross vehicle weight (RGW), or the weight prescribed in regulations under the Highway Traffic Act. Once these weights have been determined, the lower figure of these is the maximum gross allowable weight.

Drivers, operators and shippers are all responsible for the weight of the commercial vehicle and any may be charged with an offence.

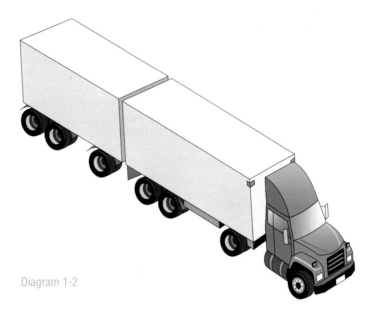

Diagram 1-2

III. A and D licence classes and requirements

Truck inspections and inspection stations

In Ontario, truck inspection stations are at various highway locations. Signs indicate whether or not a station is open. If a station is open, trucks must enter and stop for inspection.

Vehicles and loads are checked for weight, height, length, width and axle spacing. Registration permits and licences are checked to ensure that a "for hire" carrier has the authority to transport the goods carried.

Driver licences are also checked for validity and proper class of licence for the vehicle.

Drivers are required to produce documents to show that they meet regulatory and legislative requirements such as daily trip inspections, log books indicating hours worked, and proof of commercial vehicle operator registration.

Vehicles are subject to safety checks (brakes, lights, couplings, and so on).

In addition to permanent truck inspection stations, mobile inspection units may be set up for varying lengths of time in any locality.

Any police officer or appointed ministry officer may require you to drive to the nearest inspection station. If required, you must assist in the inspection of the vehicle. Inspections may be done on a highway at any time.

If you refuse or fail to proceed to a weigh scale, when required, you are guilty of an offence and liable to a fine of $200 to $1,000. You may also have your licence suspended for up to 30 days.

Also, drivers who refuse or fail to redistribute or remove part of the load, or make arrangements to do so, or obstruct any weighing, measuring or examination, are guilty of an offence and liable to a fine of $100 to $200.

Operation of commercial motor vehicles

The operator and driver of the truck are responsible to ensure that it is fit for highway use. Commercial vehicles must have Periodic Mandatory Commercial Vehicle Inspections (PMCVI). Proof of such inspections may be in the form of a decal affixed to the vehicle.

Inspection and maintenance

Drivers play an important part in making sure that trucks and buses using Ontario highways are in good operating condition. The most effective method for drivers to determine that their vehicle is in safe operating condition is to do a vehicle inspection or circle check before starting the day's trip. It is a good safety practice to repeat the vehicle inspection each time you stop, especially after a rest stop, before you continue on the trip.

In addition to being a good safety practice a circle check or trip inspection is a requirement of the Highway Traffic Act.

The ministry's role is to monitor the condition of commercial motor vehicles operating in Ontario and, when necessary, take corrective action. One method of accomplishing this task is through vehicle inspections, which can be performed by ministry enforcement staff or police officers.

In cases where serious infractions are discovered, for example out of adjustment air brakes, invalid Commercial Vehicle Operator Registration (CVOR) and overloads, the vehicle is taken out of service. For less serious infractions such as broken clearance lights the driver is required to repair the problem.

The most common reason for taking a commercial vehicle out of service is for out-of-adjustment air brakes. Other reasons include insecure loads, defective lights and tires and broken springs. It is therefore very important that drivers also complete a proper air brake pre-trip inspection as described in The Official Air Brake Handbook before starting the day's trip. In addition to being unsafe, out of adjustment airbrakes can result in a vehicle being detained and/or the operator's CVOR certificate may be cancelled or suspended.

Note: Drivers cannot adjust their own air brakes unless they have either completed an approved air brake adjustment course or they are a certified mechanic.

III. A and D licence classes and requirements

Another important component of vehicle safety is tires and wheels. The tires and wheels of a commercial vehicle must be checked as part of the pre-trip inspection to ensure they meet the safety standards. The rear tire of a motor vehicle must have more than 1.5 millimetres (0.05 in.) of tread measured in two adjacent tread grooves. The front tires of a motor vehicle with a gross vehicle rating of more than 4500 kg must have at least 3 millimetres (0.12 in.) of tread measured in two adjacent tread grooves.

Tires and wheels must be inspected daily to ensure there is the appropriate tread depth and that the wheels are securely attached. It is also a good safety practice to inspect the wheels, wheel fasteners and tires after having new tires or wheels installed. Wheel manufacturers recommend having wheel fasteners rechecked between 80 km and 160 km after installation. Wheels and tires must be installed by a qualified installer.

Loading and unloading

The Highway Traffic Act states that any load overhanging the rear of a vehicle by 1.5 m (5 ft) or more should be marked by a red light when lights are required (one-half hour before sunset to one-half hour after sunrise) and, at all other times, by a red flag or red marker.

All loads carried on a motor vehicle or trailer must be bound, covered or otherwise securely fastened or loaded so no portion of the load can fall off.

Before moving a load, drivers should know the type of cargo they are carrying. Many commodities now being hauled require safety devices for the driver such as protective bulkheads, special lading, and so on. Before starting a trip or after unloading, drivers should check that van doors are latched or that racks, tarps and other equipment are secured.

The driver is responsible to make sure the load is evenly balanced and properly secured against shifting. A cargo that breaks loose or shifts during a sudden stop or sharp turn could cause a collision.

Diagram 1-3

IV. Daily trip inspection — classes A and D

Drivers must, by law, inspect their vehicles and be capable of determining if they are in a safe operating condition. A list of items to be inspected helps make sure that all components are inspected in a minimum of time. The circle check or daily trip inspection in this book shows the absolute minimum inspection that must be performed. A driver must perform a vehicle inspection before starting the day's trip. It is also a good safety practice to do a vehicle inspection each time you stop, especially after a rest stop, before you continue on the trip. Upon identifying a safety defect, the condition of the defect must be reported to the operator as soon as possible and the safety defect must be repaired before the vehicle is operated. In addition, any defects found during the operation of the vehicle must be repaired immediately.

The circle check

Diagram 1-4 on page 21 shows a systematic circle check you should make. Details of the check can change according to the type of vehicle, but generally the principle of making a complete circle should be followed.

Some points to look out for are given in the sample.

As part of the road test, you will be asked to explain and perform the following inspections:

1. Engine — check:
- oil and coolant levels
- all drive belts and hoses
- for loose wires and leaks

2. Enter cab and:
- adjust seat and mirrors
- start engine
- check horn, wipers and all gauges and ensure that the low pressure warning device is operating
- while air pressure is building up, check emergency equipment
- when maximum pressure is gained, check for air leaks
- check all braking systems (refer to page 27)
- apply brakes, checking for pressure to drop (brake adjustment)
- turn on lights (lowbeam), put on left signal

The circle check or daily trip inspection

3. Leave cab and, starting with left front, circle clockwise, checking:

- all lights
- wheel lugs, nuts and tires
- air hoses and electric lines to trailer (class A only)
- suspension and frame
- tailgate, trailer doors or tarp tie-downs
- trailer dolly wheels (class A only)
- fifth wheel (class A only)
- dimmer switch operation, put on right signal
- check signal lights and high-beam headlights
- clean glass and mirrors

Diagram 1-4

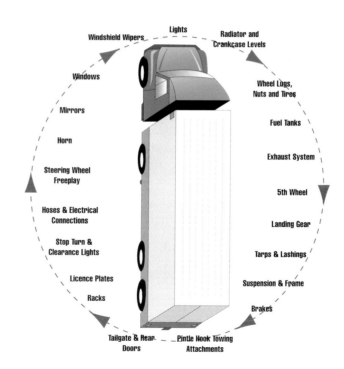

Windshield Wipers
Lights
Radiator and Crankcase Levels
Windows
Wheel Lugs, Nuts and Tires
Mirrors
Fuel Tanks
Horn
Exhaust System
Steering Wheel Freeplay
5th Wheel
Hoses & Electrical Connections
Landing Gear
Stop Turn & Clearance Lights
Tarps & Lashings
Licence Plates
Suspension & Frame
Racks
Brakes
Tailgate & Rear Doors
Pintle Hook Towing Attachments

The circle check or daily trip inspection

Uncoupling and coupling of combinations (class A only)

Uncoupling

1. Secure tractor and block trailer wheels if necessary; make certain trailer spring brakes are applied.

2. Check to see if the ground is firm enough to support landing gear. If necessary use planks or pads.

3. Lower trailer landing gear using low gear, if equipped, far enough to pick up the weight of trailer to the proper height for uncoupling, and secure the handle. Take care not to raise the trailer so high that no weight is on the fifth wheel, and avoid uncoupling with the trailer so low as to make re-coupling difficult or impossible. If the trailer has two-speed crank gear, place it in low range and stow the crank securely.

4. Release the secondary lock and pull the fifth wheel locking handle as far as it will go into the open position.

5. Start the tractor and pull ahead until the trailer upper plate slips to the lower part of the fifth wheel just above the chassis of the tractor. Stop and secure the tractor in this position.

6. Close the air lines either by cocks at the rear of the tractor cab, or the control valve on the dash.

7. Disconnect the supply or emergency air line from the trailer supply or emergency coupling; secure it to the dummy coupler on the rear of the cab.

8. Disconnect the light cord from the socket on the trailer, hang it on the rear of the cab.

9. Disconnect the service air line from the trailer service coupling, secure it to the dummy coupler on the rear of the cab.

10. Get back in the tractor and pull ahead slowly until the two units are separated.

Coupling

Be sure the fifth-wheel jaws are fully opened and the fifth wheel is tilted back so that hook-up can be made without damage. Make a visual inspection of the condition of the king pin and the fifth wheel. If the tractor is not equipped with a trailer hand valve or an emergency control valve, the trailer wheels must be blocked.

- Back the tractor so the fifth-wheel slot is in line with the trailer kingpin.
- Stop the tractor just as the fifth wheel makes contact with the trailer.
- Secure the tractor and check to see the trailer is secured against movement before coupling.

- Connect the brake lines and light cord to the trailer before coupling.
- Open cocks or actuate the control valve on the dash in the cab to charge the trailer air system.
- Release the trailer hand control valve and listen for exhausting air to determine whether the trailer brakes are operating.
- Be sure the trailer brake lines are properly connected. These are the standard colours usually used in the trucking industry:
  RED - is supply or emergency
  BLUE - is service
- Before backing under the trailer, check the height of the trailer in relation to the fifth wheel. The trailer should be at a height where moderate resistance is met as the fifth-wheel contacts the trailer plate.

- Back slowly under the trailer. See that firm contact is made between the fifth wheel and the upper plate on the trailer. Continue backing until you hear the jaws lock.

To test hook-up

Place the transmission in reverse, partially release the clutch to move the power unit backward in a short, sharp motion. This is known as "hitting the pin."

Depress the clutch and place the transmission in the lowest forward gear. If the vehicle is equipped with a trailer hand control, pull it down to set trailer brakes to keep the unit from rolling. If there is no hand control, set the trailer parking brake. Try to pull forward against the pin.

Check coupling: (visual inspection)

- Leave the cab and look under the front of the trailer to be sure the upper plate of the trailer is resting firmly on the fifth wheel. If any space appears, the coupling is not secure.
- Be sure the fifth-wheel release lever is in locked position and the secondary lock, if there is one, is engaged.
- From behind the tractor, see that the jaws are completely closed.

Raise the landing gear after checking the hook-up and before moving the unit. Be sure the gear is fully raised. If you use a two-speed crank gear, place it in low range, and stow the crank securely.

V. Hours of work

There are very specific rules regarding hours of work for drivers. These hours of work rules have been accepted Canada-wide as part of the National Safety Code and are contained in Regulation 4/93 of the Highway Traffic Act.

Some of the rules are as follows:

- Drivers may not drive a truck or bus after having driven for 13 hours or been on duty 15 hours without being off duty for eight consecutive hours.
- A driver may not drive a truck or bus after being on duty for 60 hours in seven days.
- A driver may not drive a truck or bus after being on duty for 70 hours in eight days.

- A driver may not drive a truck or bus after being on duty for 120 hours in 14 days and the driver must have been off duty for at least 24 consecutive hours before the driver totals 75 hours on duty during the period.
- A driver delayed by unexpected adverse driving conditions may exceed the allowable on duty time by two hours.

On duty is the time spent driving the vehicle or performing other duties required by the operator and include duties such as loading or unloading, or waiting for repairs or a load. A driver is considered off duty when they are not performing duties required by the operator or when they are in the sleeper berth of the truck.

Drivers are required to complete a daily written log and a daily trip inspection report containing details of the vehicles driven and hours and kilometers driven in each vehicle in addition to the results of the daily trip inspection. The driver is not required to make a written log if they are driving within a 160 km radius of the place they report to work, but the hours of limitation still apply. However, a written daily trip inspection of the vehicles must be performed within the previous 24 hours, and the driver shall carry this report and surrender it on demand.

It is important that all drivers know all laws, which may affect their job as a truck driver. Drivers should make it their business to be aware. You can contact your local ministry enforcement office for any additional information.

DRIVING — CLASSES A AND D

Starting the engine

1. Engage the parking brake, adjust the choke, depress the clutch pedal, and place the transmission in neutral.
2. Turn on the ignition, operate the starter.
3. Control the engine with the foot throttle until it is running smoothly.
4. Check the gauge for the proper oil pressure.
5. On air brake vehicles, the air pressure gauge should register sufficient pressure before moving. The audible air warning buzzer must have stopped sounding and/or the warning light must be off.

Note: For more information on air brakes, see The Official Air Brake Handbook.

Putting vehicle into motion

When starting to move, gradually release the clutch and at the same time release the hand control valve or parking brake. At the same time, the engine must be speeded up gradually on some vehicles to prevent stalling.

Brakes must be checked immediately after the vehicle is underway, within at least 15 m (50 ft).

Driving — classes A and D

Transmissions

- It is your responsibility to be thoroughly familiar with transmission shift patterns and shifting procedures. We recommend that you study the truck manufacturer's operating manual.
- When you start to move, put the vehicle in the lowest gear ratio available.
- **Do not shock-load the drive-line through rapid operation of the clutch.** Take care when applying power to move heavy loads uphill.
- Do not allow the clutch to slip: it will generate excessive heat, cause the clutch to drag and bring on premature clutch failure. Remember: co-ordinated clutch operation and smooth transmission shifting will prolong the life of any vehicle.

Some vehicles are equipped with a **clutch brake**. When driving them, the clutch pedal should not be depressed all the way to the floor when shifting, except at a stop. To re-enter low gear, the pedal should be depressed to the floor to produce an easy, quiet engagement into low gear, with the vehicle at rest.

Inter-axle differential lock

The inter-axle differential lock is used on vehicles with tandem rear axles. Differential lock is controlled by a lever or push-pull control valve on the instrument panel.

This feature can be in only two positions — lock or unlock — as indicated.

Periodically, the valve should be operated to make sure it moves freely; normally the valve should be kept in the unlock position.

Lock position should be used only when you approach conditions where one or both wheels of an axle may slip. The valve locks the differential and causes it to act as a "through drive," transmitting power equally to both axles. Avoid unnecessary use of differential lock since it will result in tire wear and axle strain.

Caution: Differential lock should not be activated when wheels are actually spinning.

Note: Proper operating instructions vary from manufacturer to manufacturer. Refer to your owner's manual for further instructions.

Brake inspection

While drivers are not expected to be able to service a disabled braking system, they should be knowledge-able enough to pinpoint the trouble. The following inspection routines should always be carried out as part of the daily trip inspection.

1. Hydraulic brakes (without power assist):

- Apply brakes moderately and hold.
- If the pedal shows a steady drop, the vehicle should be taken out of service and the system inspected professionally.

2. Hydraulic brakes (with power assist):

- With the engine stopped, pump the brake pedal several times to eliminate power assist.
- Apply brakes moderately and hold.
- Start the engine (the pedal should drop slightly and stop).
- If the pedal continues to drop or does not drop (no power assist) stop the engine. The vehicle should be taken out of service and the system inspected professionally.

Use of brakes

- Brakes should be applied with steady pressure at the beginning of a stop, then eased off as the vehicle slows. Just before the vehicle comes to a complete stop, brakes should be released enough to avoid a jerk and rebound, then applied again to hold vehicle while stopped.
- Brakes should not be fanned (alternately applied and released) except on slippery pavement where this type of braking gives better control, reduces danger of skidding and gives a shorter stop. Fanning reduces air pressure and serves no useful purpose on dry pavement and fanning on a long downhill grade may reduce air pressure below the minimum pres-sure needed for proper brake operation.

Driving — classes A and D

- Great care must be taken to avoid excessive use of brakes on long downgrades, as overheated brakes are dangerously inefficient. Drivers should use engine compression as the principal means of controlling speed on long grades.

  If possible, drivers should use the same gear in descending a long grade as they would in climbing it. Gear selection should be made before descending a grade to minimize the chance of missing a shift.
- If the low air pressure warning device operates at anytime, drivers must stop immediately in the safest available place and correct the loss of air pressure before proceeding.

- If brakes should fail on a level road, drivers should downshift and use engine compression to slow the vehicle. If a shorter stopping distance is necessary, they should use the tractor and trailer emergency brakes, if fitted, to stop. The vehicle should not be driven until repairs have been made.
- In a combination of vehicles such as a truck-tractor and semi-trailer, trailer brakes are applied with the truck brakes using the foot control valve. This is known as balanced braking. The pressure applied on both the trailer and the truck-tractor brakes is the same. Trailer brakes may be applied independently by using the trailer hand valve. The amount of pressure on the trailer brakes during a foot valve application may be increased by pulling harder on the hand valve.

- Exercise care in braking a combination of vehicles on wet or slippery surfaces, or on a curve. Overbraking in these circumstances can result in skidding or jack-knifing. If the tractor is jack-knifing, i.e. if the tractor rear wheels slide sideways, apply the trailer brakes only. If the trailer is jack-knifing, i.e. if the trailer rear wheels slide sideways, release all brakes and apply power.
- Emergency (spring brakes) are installed on newer equipment. They apply automatically when the air pressure in the system drops below a predetermined level, usually at 138-311 kPa (25-45 psi).

Note: If you plan to operate a vehicle equipped with air brakes, refer to The Official Air Brake Handbook for further information.

Parking

To ensure that a unit will stay in position when parked, take the following precautions to prevent a runaway vehicle.

1. Set parking brakes.
2. Block the unit.
3. Under no circumstances should a driver use the trailer hand valve, or the tractor protection valve to hold a parked unit.

Driver conduct

Today's truck drivers are among the highway's most visible citizens, and the motoring public tends to criticize some of their driving practices. So it's up to them to influence the public's opinion. Be a defensive driver — anticipate what other drivers might do and compensate for them.

1. **Obstructing traffic:** Slowing down on hills is often unavoidable, but good drivers can reduce the delay to faster vehicles by being aware of the following traffic and pulling off the roadway when it is safe to do so, allowing faster traffic to pass. Never use your left-turn signals to tell following motorists it is safe to pass. It is against the law and tends to confuse other drivers, who may think you are signaling a left turn or lane change.

2. **Improper passing:** Some truck drivers switch on their turn signals and immediately pull out into traffic when the traffic stream is too close and dense. Another complaint is the practice of pulling out to pass another large vehicle on a multiple lane highway when the difference in speed is so small that the manoeuvre obstructs following traffic for an unreasonable period of time. Avoid these errors.

3. **Bluffing:** Drivers who use the large size of their vehicles to intimidate others and force their way through traffic may create serious hazards.

4. **Following:** When a number of trucks pull onto a highway after a stop, drivers should do so at intervals that will allow them to leave sufficient space. Commercial motor vehicles must maintain a minimum distance of at least 60 m (200 ft) between themselves and other vehicles when on a highway at a speed exceeding 60 km/h (40 mph) except when overtaking and passing another motor vehicle.

Driving — classes A and D

5. Sharing the road with smaller vehicles:

Motorcycles, mopeds, motor assisted bicycles and bicycles are harder to see because of their size. Drivers of these vehicles may make sudden moves because of uneven road surfaces or poor weather conditions. And because they are less protected, they are more likely to be injured in a collision.

Drivers of motorcycles, mopeds, motor assisted bicycles and bicycles must obey the same rules of the road as car, truck and bus drivers. However, mopeds and bicycles that cannot keep up with traffic should drive as close as possible to the right edge of the road. For safety, cyclists should ride at least one metre away from parked vehicles and at least one-half metre away from the curb to avoid debris, potholes and sewer grates. The cyclist has the right to use the whole lane.

Motorcycles use a full lane; treat them like other vehicles when driving. Since many motorcycle turn signals do not automatically shut off, be careful when turning left in front of an oncoming motorcycle with its turn signal on. Make sure the motorcyclist is turning and not going through your path having forgotten to switch off the turn signal.

Diagram 2-1

Diagram 2-2

6. Sharing the road with pedestrians:

Pay special attention to pedestrians, whether they are crossing roads in traffic, walking or jogging alongside roads, or using crosswalks or pedestrian crossings. Elderly pedestrians or those with disabilities need extra caution and courtesy from drivers, as they may be slow in crossing the road. Be alert for pedestrians who are blind, visually impaired, hearing impaired, people in wheel chairs or people walking slowly due to some other physical impairment and give them appropriate consideration. Pedestrians who are blind or visually impaired may use *a white cane or guide dog* to help them travel safely along sidewalks and across intersections. Caution signs are posted in some areas where there is a special need for drivers to be alert.

Some streetcar stops have a special safety island or zone for passengers getting on and off. Pass these safety islands and zones at a reasonable speed. Always be ready in case pedestrians make sudden or unexpected moves.

7. Yielding the right-of-way:

There are times when you must yield the right-of-way. This means you must let another person go first. Here are some rules about when you must yield the right-of-way:

- At an intersection without signs or lights, you must yield the right-of-way to any vehicle approaching from the right (Diagram 2-3).

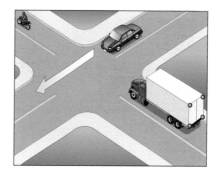

Diagram 2-3

Driving — classes A and D

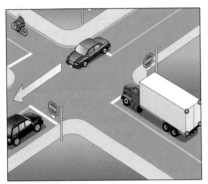

Diagram 2-4

Diagram 2-5

Diagram 2-6

- At an intersection with stop signs at all corners, you must yield the right-of-way to the first vehicle to come to a complete stop. If two vehicles stop at the same time, the vehicle on the left must yield to the vehicle on the right.

- At any intersection where you want to turn left or right, you must yield the right-of-way. If you are turning left, you must wait for approaching traffic to pass or turn and for pedestrians in your path to cross. If you are turning right, you must wait for pedestrians to cross.

- A yield sign means you must slow down or stop if necessary and yield the right-of-way to traffic in the intersection or on the intersecting road.

When entering a road from a private road or driveway, you must yield to vehicles on the road and pedestrians on the sidewalk.

Diagram 2-7

- You must yield the right-of-way to pedestrians crossing at specially marked pedestrian crossings or crossovers.

Remember, signalling does not give you the right-of-way. You must make sure the way is clear.

10 WAYS YOU CAN HELP MAKE ONTARIO'S ROADS THE SAFEST IN NORTH AMERICA

1. Don't drink and drive. Don't drive when you're taking medication that will affect your driving.

2. Always wear your seat belt.

3. Obey the speed limits. Slow down when road and weather conditions are poor.

4. Don't take risks: don't cut people off in traffic, make sudden lane changes or run yellow lights.

5. Don't drive when you're tired, upset or sick.

6. If you're in doubt, let the other driver go first — yield the right-of-way.

7. Keep a safe distance between your vehicle and the one ahead.

8. Avoid distractions such as loud music and CB radios.

9. Check your mirrors frequently; always check your blind spot before you change lanes.

10. Check traffic in all directions before going into an intersection.

Driving — classes A and D

Stopping

Knowing how to stop safely and properly is an important driving skill. Good drivers see stops ahead, check their mirrors and begin braking early, stopping smoothly. Braking is easier when you sit properly. Use your right foot for both brake and gas pedals so you won't step on both pedals at the same time or flash your brake lights unnecessarily. Press the brake pedal firmly and evenly.

Shift into a lower gear when going down long, steep hills. This will help control your speed and you won't have to brake as sharply. Downshift before starting downhill since it may not be possible afterwards. As a guide, you should be in the same gear going downhill as uphill.

You must come to a complete stop at all stop signs and red traffic lights. Stop at the stop line if it is marked on the pavement (Diagram 2-8).

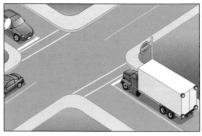

Diagram 2-8

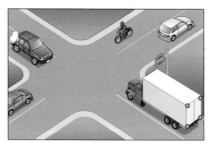

Diagram 2-9

If there is no stop line, stop at the crosswalk, marked or not. If there is no crosswalk, stop at the edge of the sidewalk. If there is no sidewalk, stop at the edge of the intersection (Diagram 2-9). Wait until the way is clear before entering the intersection.

Stopping at railway crossings

All railway crossings on public roads in Ontario are marked with large red and white 'X' signs. Watch for these signs and be prepared to stop. You may also see signs warning of railway crossings ahead. On private roads, railway crossings may not be marked, so watch carefully.

As you come to a crossing, slow down, listen and look both ways to make sure the way is clear before crossing the tracks. If a train is coming, stop at least five metres from the nearest rail. Do not cross the track until you are sure all trains have passed.

Some railway crossings have flashing signal lights and some use gates or barriers to keep drivers from crossing the tracks when a train is coming.

At a railway crossing where the signal lights are flashing, stop at least five metres from the nearest rail. Do not cross until the signals stop flashing. If the crossing has a gate or barrier, wait until it rises or opens before crossing. It is dangerous and illegal to drive around, under or through a railway gate or barrier while it is being opened or closed.

Buses and other public vehicles are required to stop at railway crossings that are not protected by gates or signal lights. School buses must stop at railway crossings whether or not they are protected by gates or signal lights.

Watch for these buses and be prepared to stop behind them.

Be careful in heavy traffic not to drive onto a railway crossing if you may have to stop on the tracks.

Always make sure there is enough space to drive across the tracks completely before you begin to cross.

Diagram 2-10

Driving — classes A and D

Stopping at school crossings

You must stop for school crossing guards guiding children across a road. These guards carry red and white stop signs. Drivers who don't stop can be fined.

Stopping for school buses

All school buses in Ontario, whatever their size, are chrome yellow and display the words 'School Bus'.

No matter what direction you are travelling in, you must stop whenever you approach a stopped school bus with its upper alternating red lights flashing, unless you are on a road with a median. In that case only vehicles coming from behind must stop. (A median is a raised, lowered or earth strip dividing a road where vehicles travel in both directions.) Coming from the opposite direction, stop at a safe distance for children to get off the bus and cross the road in front of you. If you are coming from behind the bus, stop at least 20 metres away. Do not go until the bus moves or the lights have stopped flashing.

You must obey the school bus law on any road, no matter how many lanes or what the speed limit. Be prepared to stop for a school bus at any time, not just within school hours.

As well as the upper alternating red flashing lights, school buses use a stop sign arm on the driver's side of the bus. This arm, a standard stop sign with alternating flashing red lights at

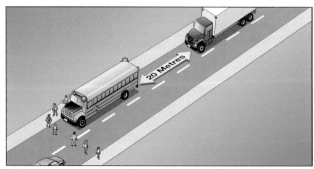

Diagram 2-11

Diagram 2-12

top and bottom, swings out after the upper alternating red lights begin to flash. Do not go until the arm folds away and all lights stop flashing.

If you don't stop for a school bus, you can be fined $400 to $2,000 and get six demerit points for a first offence. If you break the rule a second time within five years, the penalty is a fine of $1,000 to $4,000 and six demerit points. You could also go to jail for up to six months.

Watch for school buses near railway crossings. All school buses must stop at all railway crossings. The upper alternating red lights are not used for these stops, so be alert.

Stopping for pedestrian crossings

Pedestrian crossings — also called "crossovers" — let pedestrians safely cross roads where there are no traffic lights. Always watch for pedestrians and people using wheelchairs near these crossings. At some crossings, pedestrians can push a button to make overhead yellow

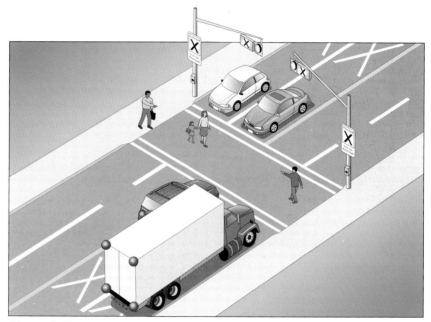

Diagram 2-13

lights flash; at all crossings, pedestrians should point across the road to show they want to cross. Drivers, including cyclists, must stop and let all pedestrians cross. Once people

have cleared your side of the road you can go with caution.

Never pass another vehicle that has stopped to let people cross the road.

Driving — classes A and D

Clearances

Drivers of larger vehicles must know their vehicle's height and width and watch for and obey clearance signs on bridges and underpasses. They must also remember that road repairs, rough roads, ice, floods may cause difficulty where clearance is otherwise normally adequate.

Drivers must follow instructions on signs posted where dangerous conditions exist and obey regulations that ban trucks on certain highways, at certain times or on certain days.

Turns and steering

Turning a large vehicle requires more care and knowledge than turning a passenger car. Besides observing the general turn rules outlined in The Official Driver's Handbook, operators of large vehicles must keep other factors in mind. For example, during a given turn of the steering wheel, the rear wheels follow a shorter path than those up front. Allow this on all turns so that the vehicle doesn't strike another vehicle or stationary object.

Steering (forward) and off-track

The rear wheels of the vehicle do not pivot and therefore will not follow the same path as the front wheels. The greater the distance (wheel base) between the front wheels and the rear wheels of the vehicle, the greater the amount of "off-track." The off-track path has a shorter radius than the path of the front wheels.

On the open highway, you must lead your turning arc of the front wheels according to the sharpness of the curve and the amount of off-track of your vehicle (Diagram 2-14). A curve to the right requires keeping the front wheels close to the centre line to prevent dropping the rear wheels off the pavement. A curve to the left requires keeping the front wheels close to the right edge of the pavement to prevent the rear wheels from crossing into the other traffic lane.

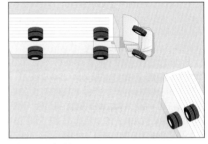

Diagram 2-14

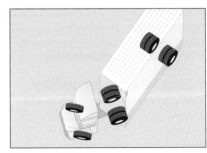

Diagram 2-15

A combination vehicle such as a semi-trailer unit has an off-track of the rear wheels of the tractor unit, and a greater off-track again of the rear wheels of a semi.

The combination unit of a truck-tractor and semi-trailer has different turning characteristics. These units have a turning radius and off-track pattern within each unit, but the amount of off-track depends upon the length of the combination and the wheel base of the units **(Diagram 2-15)**.

Whenever possible, turns must be made from the proper lanes. When it becomes necessary for the driver to direct the vehicle over lane lines or centre lines to negotiate sharp turns, it is the driver's responsibility to be sure that the movement can be made safely, without interfering with other traffic.

Right turns

Right turns at intersections with vehicles that have a lot of off-track, require the driver to lead the turning arc according to the amount of off-track. Running the rear wheels of the unit over curbs and sidewalks not only results in tire damage, but is hazardous to pedestrians. Power poles, sign posts or lamp standards mounted close to the curb at intersections are also hazards.

Generally it is better to use more space from the road you are leaving than to use more space from the road you are entering.

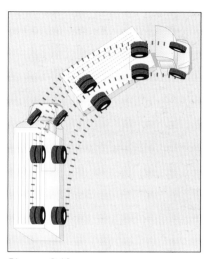

Diagram 2-16

Driving — classes A and D

If streets are narrow, you will need to proceed well into the intersection before beginning a turn. It may be necessary to travel over the centre line or into the second traffic lane of the street entered. Drivers must use extreme caution and ensure the movement can be made safely.

When it becomes necessary to "block" off another traffic lane, make sure that smaller vehicles, motorcycles, or cyclists are not attempting to move up along the right side of your vehicle. The critical point is reached when the tractor is at the sharpest point of the turn in relation to the trailer, because vision through the right rear view mirror is limited.

Left turns

Truck drivers must be aware of and allow for any off-track when making a left turn. Unless the driver uses his or her left outside mirror to monitor the trailer's path, the trailer might hit either a vehicle or a sign post on an island. It is necessary to turn the vehicle in a wide arc before bringing it back to its proper position after a left turn, just right of the centre line. Then as the speed is increased, the driver can move, when it is safe, to the right lane.

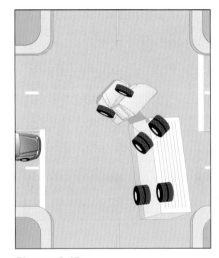

Diagram 2-17

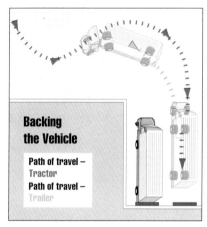

**Backing
the Vehicle**

Path of travel –
Tractor
Path of travel –
Trailer

Diagram 2-18

Backing

Because of the hazards of backing, avoid it when possible. Planning your route in advance may eliminate the need for backing. If necessary, drive around the block if it will avoid backing around a corner. Drive out into traffic rather than backing into traffic. Avoid entering the path of a reversing vehicle and do not stop or park behind a vehicle that may soon be reversed.

Backing a single unit vehicle is similar to backing a passenger vehicle. However, backing a tractor with a semi-trailer requires some practice.

- Get out and walk around the vehicle to examine the area into which you must back. Look for overhead obstacles or wires, side clearances, pedestrians or objects in your path of travel.
- Whenever possible, back from the driver's side and start backing from as close to the dock as reasonably possible. Although you may start with the vehicle in a straight line, it may be less difficult if you position your vehicle so that the trailer is angled in the direction you want it to take.
- Use both rear view mirrors. Even with two mirrors, vision is limited. There is always a blind spot to the rear that a mirror cannot reflect.
- Back SLOWLY, in an S shaped curve, by first turning the tractor wheels in the opposite direction to that in which you want to move the rear of the trailer. Before you reach a jack-knife position, the tractor must "follow" in a track related to the track of the trailer (forming the bottom portion of the "S").
- Moving slowly, the tractor should "follow" the trailer until both tractor and trailer are straight. Then continue slowly to ease up to the dock.

Driving — classes A and D

A responsible guide or flagperson can help you by watching the area into which you are backing, keeping an eye on your blind zone. This person should stand in a position to see both you and the area to the rear of your vehicle clearly, and warn you if pedestrians or vehicles move into your path as you back. This can help you make an easy approach to the dock.

Remember that back-up alarm devices do not relieve the driver of responsibility when reversing.

PRECAUTIONS

I. Precautions

Observe the laws governing the operation of a motor vehicle scrupulously and make every effort to follow good driving practice and safety rules.

- Back a truck with the utmost care and caution. Use all rear view mirrors, turn and look back and, if possible, have someone give you directions. Back slowly and cautiously and watch traffic conditions around the vehicle at all times.
- Bad weather requires changing your driving procedures. Exercise exceptional care in such conditions.
- Adjust your speed to meet road, weather and traffic conditions.
- Never load a truck beyond its licensed capacity.
- Avoid situations that call for quick stops.
- Never allow an unauthorized person to occupy the driver's seat, operate the truck or any of its controls.

I. Precautions

HIGHWAY HYPNOSIS

Driving for a long time can be boring, especially at night or when you drive at the same speed for long distances. You can become "hypnotized" where everything seems to float by and you pay less attention to what is happening around you. You may even fall asleep.

You can help prevent highway hypnosis by following a few simple suggestions:
- Don't eat a heavy meal before you drive.
- Wear comfortable clothing.
- Talk with your passengers, but not to the point of distraction.
- Keep your eyes moving and check your mirrors often.
- Take an interest in all road signs and traffic around you.
- If possible, take regular coffee or walking breaks.
- Don't try to drive too far in one day.
- Avoid driving during your normal sleeping hours.
- Keep the temperature in your vehicle cool.

If you do start to become drowsy, do something different immediately. Open a window, talk out loud, move your body around a bit. If possible, stop at the next service centre or rest area and take a short walk or have a coffee and eat a light snack. If you don't feel any more alert, consider finding a place to sleep for an hour or for the night.

II. Driving at night and in bad weather

At night and in weather conditions such as rain, snow or fog, you cannot see as far ahead, even with headlights. Slow down when driving at night, especially on unlit roads, and whenever weather conditions reduce your visibility.

Overdriving your headlights

You are overdriving your headlights when your stopping distance is farther than you can see with your headlights. This is a dangerous thing to do because you may not give yourself enough room to make a safe stop. Reflective road signs can mislead you as well, making you believe you can see farther than you really can. This may cause you to overdrive your headlights if you are not careful.

Glare

Glare is dazzling light that makes it hard for you to see and be aware of what others around you are doing. It can be a problem on sunny and overcast days, depending on the angle of the sun's rays and your surroundings. Glare can also be a problem at night when you face bright headlights or see them reflected in your mirrors.

When meeting oncoming vehicles with bright headlights at night, look up and beyond and slightly to the right of the oncoming lights. In daytime glare, use your sun visor or use a pair of good quality sunglasses. When you enter a tunnel on a bright day, slow down to let your eyes adjust to the reduced light. Remove your sunglasses and turn on your headlights.

Cut down glare at night by following the rules of the road for vehicle lights. Use your lowbeam headlights within 150 metres (500 ft) of an oncoming vehicle or when following a vehicle within 60 metres (200 ft). On country roads, switch to lowbeams when you come to a curve or hilltop so you can see oncoming headlights and won't blind oncoming drivers. If you can't see any headlights, switch back to highbeams.

II. Driving at night and in bad weather

TIPS FOR SAFE DRIVING IN FOG

Before you drive — and during your trip — check weather forecasts. If there is a fog warning, delay your trip until it clears, if possible. If you are caught driving in fog, follow these safe driving tips:

DO:
- Slow down gradually and drive at a speed that suits the conditions.
- Make sure the full lighting system of your vehicle is turned on.
- Use your lowbeam headlights. Highbeams reflect off the moisture droplets in the fog, making it harder to see.
- If you have fog lights on your vehicle, use them, in addition to your low beams. They could save your life.
- Be patient. Avoid passing, changing lanes and crossing traffic.
- Use pavement markings to help guide you. Use the right edge of the road as a guide, rather than the centre line.
- Increase your following distance. You will need extra distance to brake safely.
- Look and listen for any hazards that may be ahead.
- Reduce the distractions in your vehicle. For example, turn off the cell phone ... your full attention is required.
- Watch for any electronically operated warning signs.
- Keep looking as far ahead as possible.
- Keep your windows and mirrors clean. Use your defroster and wipers to maximize your vision.
- If the fog is too dense to continue, pull completely off the road and try to position your vehicle in an area protected from other traffic. Turn on your emergency flashers and set out warning devices (see page 57).

DON'T:

- Don't stop on the travelled portion of the road. You could become the first link in a chain-reaction collision.
- Don't speed up suddenly, even if the fog seems to be clearing. You could find yourself suddenly back in fog.
- Don't speed up to pass a vehicle moving slowly or to get away from a vehicle that is following too closely.

REMEMBER:

- Watch your speed. You may be going faster than you think. If so, reduce speed gradually.
- Leave a safe braking distance between you and the vehicle ahead.
- Remain calm and patient. Don't pass other vehicles or speed up suddenly.
- Don't stop on the road. If visibility is decreasing rapidly, pull off the road into a safe parking area and wait for the fog to lift.
- When visibility is reduced, use your lowbeams.

Fog

Fog is a thin layer of cloud resting on the ground. Fog reduces visibility for drivers, resulting in difficult driving conditions.

The best thing to do is to avoid driving in fog. Check weather forecasts and if there is a fog warning, delay your trip until it clears. If that is not possible or you get caught driving in fog, there are a number of safe driving tips you should follow. See Tips for Safe Driving in Fog on pages 46 to 47.

If visibility is decreasing rapidly, move off the road and into a safe parking area to wait for the fog to lift.

II. Driving at night and in bad weather

Rain

Rain makes road surfaces slippery, especially as the first drops fall. With more rain, tires make less contact with the road. If there is too much water or if you are going too fast, your tires may ride on top of the water, like water skis. This is called hydroplaning. When this happens, control becomes very difficult. Make sure you have good tires with deep tread, and slow down when the road is wet.

Rain also reduces visibility. Drive slow enough to be able to stop within the distance you can see. Make sure your windshield wipers are in good condition. If your wiper blades do not clean the windshield without streaking, replace them.

In rain, try to drive on clear sections of road. Look ahead and plan your movements. Smooth steering, braking and accelerating will reduce the chance of skids. Leave more space between you and the vehicle

ahead in case you have to stop. This will also help you to avoid spray from the vehicle ahead that can make it even harder to see.

Avoid driving in puddles. A puddle can hide a large pothole that could damage your vehicle or its suspension, or flatten a tire. The spray of water could splash nearby pedestrians or drown your engine, causing it to stall. Water can also make your brakes less effective.

Flooded roads

Avoid driving on flooded roads — water may prevent your brakes from working. If you must drive through a flooded stretch of road, test your brakes afterwards to dry them out.

Test your brakes **when it is safe to do so** by stopping quickly and firmly. Make sure the vehicle stops in a straight line, without pulling to one side. The brake pedal should feel firm and secure, not spongy — that's a sign of trouble.

If you still feel a pulling to one side or a spongy brake pedal even after the brakes are dry, you should take the vehicle in for repair immediately.

Skids

A skid happens when your wheels slide out of control on a slippery surface. Skids can involve the front, rear or all wheels and can cause your vehicle to jack-knife. Most skids result from driving too fast for road or traffic conditions. Sudden, hard braking, going too fast around a corner or accelerating too quickly can cause your vehicle to skid or roll over.

Once in a skid, steer in the direction of the skid. To do this, look where you want your vehicle to go and steer toward that spot. Be careful not to oversteer. If you are on ice, skidding in a straight line, step on the clutch or shift to neutral.

Threshold Braking — Threshold braking should bring you to a reasonably quick controlled stop in your own lane, even in slippery conditions. Brake as hard as you can without locking up or skidding the wheels. Press down on the brake pedal, trying to get as much braking power as possible. Then, if you feel any of the wheels locking up, release the brake pressure slightly and re-apply. Don't pump the brakes. Continue braking this way until you have brought the vehicle to a complete stop. Some vehicles have anti-lock brake systems that give you a maximum threshold stop automatically.

Anti-lock brakes — If your vehicle has an anti-lock braking system, practice emergency braking to understand how your vehicle will react. It is a good idea to practise doing this under controlled conditions with a qualified driving instructor.

Anti-lock braking systems, which are also called ABS, are designed to sense the speed of the wheels on a vehicle. An abnormal drop in wheel speed, which indicates potential wheel lock, causes the brake force to be reduced to that wheel. This is how the anti-lock braking system prevents tire skid and the accompanying loss of steering control. This improves vehicle safety during heavy brake use or when braking with poor traction.

Although anti-lock braking systems help to prevent wheel lock, you should not expect the stopping distance for your vehicle to be shortened. Under normal driving conditions, on clean dry roads, you will notice no difference between vehicles with anti-lock braking and vehicles without anti-lock braking.

Some drivers, unfamiliar with anti-lock braking, are surprised by the vibration that happens when they brake hard in an emergency. Make sure you know what to expect so you can react quickly and effectively in an emergency.

Snow
Snow may be hard-packed and slippery as ice. It can also be rutted, full of hard tracks and gullies. Or it can be smooth and soft. Look ahead and anticipate what you must do based on the conditions. Slow down on rutted snowy roads. Avoid sudden steering, braking or accelerating that could cause a skid.

Whiteouts
Blowing snow may create whiteouts where snow completely blocks your view of the road. When blowing snow is forecast, drive only if necessary and with extreme caution.

II. Driving at night and in bad weather

TIPS FOR DRIVING IN BLOWING SNOW AND WHITEOUT CONDITIONS

Before you drive — and during your trip — check weather forecasts and road reports. If there are weather warnings, or reports of poor visibility and driving conditions, delay your trip until conditions improve, if possible. If you get caught driving in blowing snow or a whiteout, follow these safe driving tips:

DO:
- Slow down gradually and drive at a speed that suits the conditions.
- Make sure the full lighting system of your vehicle is turned on.
- Be patient. Avoid passing, changing lanes and crossing traffic.
- Increase your following distance. You will need extra space to brake safely.
- Stay alert. Keep looking as far ahead as possible.
- Reduce the distractions in your vehicle. Your full attention is required.
- Keep your windows and mirrors clean. Use defroster and wipers to maximize your vision.
- Try to get off the road when visibility is near zero. Pull into a safe parking area if possible.

DON'T:
- Don't stop on the travelled portion of the road. You could become the first link in a chain-reaction collision.
- Don't attempt to pass a vehicle moving slowly or speed up to get away from a vehicle that is following too closely.

REMEMBER:

- Watch your speed. You may be going faster than you think. If so, reduce speed gradually.
- Leave a safe braking distance between you and the vehicle ahead.
- Stay alert, remain calm and be patient.
- If visibility is decreasing rapidly, do not stop on the road. Look for an opportunity to pull off the road into a safe parking area and wait for conditions to improve.
- If you become stuck or stranded in severe weather, stay with your vehicle for warmth and safety until help arrives. Slightly open a window for ventilation. Run your motor sparingly. Use your emergency flashers.
- Be prepared and carry a winter driving survival kit that includes items such as warm clothing, non-perishable energy foods, flashlight, shovel, and blanket.

Ice

As temperatures drop below freezing, wet roads become icy. Sections of road in shaded areas or on bridges and overpasses freeze first. It is important to look ahead, slow down and anticipate.

If the road ahead looks like black and shiny asphalt, be suspicious. It may be covered with a thin layer of ice known as black ice. Generally, asphalt in the winter should look gray-white in colour. If you think there may be black ice ahead, slow down and be careful.

III. Dealing with particular situations

Snow plows

Snow removal vehicles are equipped with flashing blue lights that can be seen from 150 metres (500 ft). A flashing blue light can only be used on snow removal vehicles.

Flashing blue lights warn you of wide and slow-moving vehicles. Some snow plows have a wing that extends as far as three metres to the right of the vehicle. On freeways, several snow plows may be staggered across the road, clearing all lanes at the same time by passing a ridge of snow from plow to plow. Do not try to pass between them. This is extremely dangerous because there is not enough room to pass safely, and the ridge of wet snow can throw your vehicle out of control.

Workers on the road

Be extra careful when driving through construction zones and areas where people are working on or near the road. When approaching a construction zone, slow down and obey all warning signs and people who are directing traffic through the area. In the construction zone, drive carefully and adjust your speed and driving to suit the conditions. Obey posted speed limits, do not change lanes, be ready for sudden stops and watch for workers and construction vehicles on the road and give them more room to ensure everyone's safety.

Traffic control people are used at work zones to control vehicle traffic and prevent conflicts between construction activity and traffic. Whether you are driving during the day or at night, watch for traffic control people and follow their instructions.

Treat people working on roads with respect and be patient if traffic is delayed. Sometimes traffic in one direction must wait while vehicles from the other lane pass through a detour. If your lane is blocked and no one is directing traffic, yield to the driver coming from the opposite direction. When the way is clear, move slowly and carefully around the obstacle.

Animals on the road

You may come upon farm animals or wild animals on the road, especially in farming areas and in the northern parts of the province. Animal crossing signs warn drivers where there is a known danger of moose, deer or cattle stepping onto the road, but animals may appear anywhere. Always be alert for animals and ready to react.

Look well ahead. At night, use your highbeams where possible. When you see an animal, brake or slow down if you can without risk to vehicles behind you. If there is no traffic and no danger of colliding with any other object, steer around the animal, staying in control of your vehicle.

In some areas of the province, horse-drawn carriages may use the road. Be prepared to share the road with them.

Cellular phones and CB radios

Cellular phones and CB radios can be important safety aids for drivers. Many people use their phones or radios to report crimes and collisions and for personal safety when they are lost or their vehicles break down. But using a cellular phone or CB radio while driving takes a driver's attention from the business of driving. Distracted drivers are more likely to make a driving error or to react too slowly.

As more and more people use cellular phones, it is important that they be used safely. You should use your cellular phone only when you are parked. If you are driving and your phone rings, let your cellular voice mail service take the call and listen to the message later when you are parked. If you must use a cellular phone when driving, use a hands-free microphone. Make sure your phone is easy to see and reach and that you know how to use it. Use voice-activated or speed dialing and never take notes while driving.

Currently, there is no law against using CB radios or cellular phones while driving, but you can be charged with dangerous or careless driving if you cause a collision while using a cellular phone.

Driver distractions

Driving is a job that requires your full attention every time you get behind the wheel. As a driver you must always remember to reduce distractions and focus on the your driving. Your first responsibility is to road safety!

There are a number of possible driver distractions including:
- **Using technology devices such as cell phones, laptops or hand-held organizers**
- **Reading maps, directions or other material**
- **Grooming (combing hair, putting on make-up or shaving)**
- **Eating or drinking**
- **Taking notes**
- **Talking with passengers**
- **Tending to children or pets**
- **Adjusting the controls in your vehicle (radio, CD player or climate control)**

III. Dealing with particular situations

Careless driving is a serious offence. Police can charge drivers with careless driving, if drivers do not pay full attention to their driving. If you are convicted of careless driving, you will get six demerit points, a fine up to $1,000 and/or six months in jail. In some cases, your licence may be suspended for up to two years. **This is one of Ontario's toughest rules of the road.**

TIPS TO REDUCE DRIVER DISTRACTIONS:

- Attend to personal grooming and plan your route before you leave.
- Identify and preset your vehicle's climate control, radio and/or CD Player.
- Make it a habit to pull over and park to use your cell phone, or have a passenger take the call or let it go to your voice mail.
- Put reading material out of sight if you are tempted to read.
- Do not engage in emotional or complex conversations. Stress can also affect your driving performance.
- When you are hungry or thirsty, take a break from driving.

Remember to focus on your driving at all times. A split-second distraction behind the wheel can result in injury or even death.

Emergency vehicles

If you hear the bell or siren of a police, fire, ambulance or public utility emergency vehicle, or see its lights flashing, you must get out of the way. On a two-way road, stop as close as possible to the right-hand side of the road and clear of any intersection. On a one-way road with more than two lanes, stop as close as possible to the nearest edge of the road and clear of any intersection. Wait until the emergency vehicle has passed.

It is illegal to follow an on-duty fire vehicle or ambulance within 150 metres (500 ft) in any lane going in the same direction.

Some volunteer firefighters use a flashing green light if they have to use their personal vehicles to respond to a fire. Courteous drivers yield the right-of-way to these vehicles.

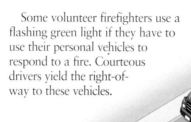

IV. Dealing with emergencies

Emergency warning devices

Every commercial motor vehicle, on a provincial highway from one-half hour before sunset to one-half hour after sunrise, must have a sufficient number of:

- flares, lamps, or lanterns capable of continuously producing two warning lights, each visible from a distance of at least 150 m (500 ft) for at least eight hours, or
- portable reflectors, during the time when lights are required

Whenever any commercial motor vehicle or trailer is disabled during those hours and the vehicle cannot immediately be removed from the roadway, the driver is required to light flares, lamps or lanterns and place them or portable reflectors on the highway until they are no longer required. One of the devices must be approximately 30 m (100 ft) in front of the vehicle and one approximately 30 m (100 ft) to the rear and visible from at least 150 m (500 ft).

Even during daylight hours, if visibility is limited by fog, rain or snow, warning devices should be used.

Hills, curves, etc: You must not park or leave a vehicle on a roadway unless there is a clear view for at least 125 m (400 ft) in both directions. Whenever the view of a stopped vehicle is blocked by a hill, curve or other obstruction within 150 m (500 ft), an additional warning signal should be placed to give ample warning to other highway users.

Use caution in placing flares where fuel or flammable material has leaked.

Breakdown procedure

If a truck stalls or breaks down on the highway, the driver should quickly and calmly take the necessary actions to safeguard the vehicle and other motorists.

1. The truck should be brought to a stop as far off the roadway as safely possible.
2. Flares, lamps, lanterns or portable reflectors should be set out at a distance of approximately 30 m (100 ft) in advance of the vehicle and at a distance of approximately 30 m (100 ft) to the rear of the vehicle and visible for a distance of at least 150 m (500 ft).

Fire Precautions

Commercial vehicle drivers should know how to prevent fires and have a basic knowledge of fire fighting techniques. It's also essential to know what types of extinguisher or retardants to use on different types of fires.

Class A: fires include burning wood, paper, textiles, tires, etc.

Class B: fires include grease, oil, gasoline, solvents, paints, etc.

Class C: fires are those occurring in live electrical equipment

Class D: fires include burning metals such as magnesium, sodium, potassium etc. Only special compounds suitable to the combustible metal involved should be used to extinguish fires on these materials

Use all extinguishers according to the manufacturer's instructions.

Some of the common causes for truck fires are:

- Running with a soft tire. Tire pressures should be checked at least every 160 km (100 miles);
- Overheated brakes, either from misuse or maladjustment. Check hub temperatures every time tires are checked;
- Leaking fuel system, carburetor, pump, filter, tanks or lines;
- Unequal distribution of load, causing trailer to lean and rub on tires;
- Careless smoking habits. Lighted cigarettes and cigars should always be butted in ash-trays, never thrown out windows. Never smoke while loading or unloading;
- Blocked air vents in a heated van can sometimes cause an explosion;
- Carelessly placed flares, lamps or fuses used in an emergency;
- Short circuits in the electrical system.

There are various other reasons for fires, such as leaking exhaust systems or those that have been installed too close to fuel lines or wooden body parts. Occasionally, spontaneous combustion may occur in a van or trailer. Drivers must always know the nature of their cargoes, so necessary fire control precautions can be taken.

IV. Dealing with emergencies

When a fire occurs:

1. Stop the vehicle in a safe position away from buildings and other vehicles.
2. If it is a combination unit, uncouple the unit if possible.
3. If the fire occurs in or near a town, contact the fire department. Tell them what type of material is burning.
4. Based on the type of fire concerned, take all possible steps to extinguish it.
5. If the fire is thought to be due to a short-circuit, remove battery cables.
6. If the cargo is of an explosive nature, stop traffic and warn spectators to stay back.

In a collision where someone is injured

St. John Ambulance recommends that all drivers carry a well-stocked first aid kit and know how to use it. Think about reading a book about first aid or sign up for a first aid course. It could mean the difference between life and death in a collision.

Every driver involved in a collision must stay at the scene or return to it immediately and give all possible assistance. If you are not personally involved in a collision, you should stop to offer help if police or other help has not arrived.

In a collision with injuries, possible fuel leaks or serious vehicle damage, stay calm and follow these steps:

1. Call for help or have someone else call. By law, you must report any collision to the police when there are injuries or damage to vehicles or other property exceeding $1,000.
2. Turn off all engines and turn on emergency flashers. Set up warning signals or flares and have someone warn approaching drivers.
3. Do not let anyone smoke, light a match or put flares near any vehicle in case of a fuel leak. If any of the vehicles is on fire, get the people out and make sure everyone is well out of the way. If there is no danger of fire or explosion, leave injured people where they are until trained medical help arrives.

4. If you are trained in first aid, treat injuries in the order of urgency, within the level of your training. For example, clear the person's airway to restore breathing, give rescue breathing or stop bleeding by applying pressure with a clean cloth.

5. If you are not trained in first aid, use common sense. For example, people in collisions often go into shock. Cover the person with a jacket or blanket to reduce the effects of shock.

6. Stay with injured people until help arrives.

7. Disabled vehicles on the road may be a danger to you and other drivers. Do what you can to make sure everyone involved in a collision is kept safe.

In a collision where no one is injured

Follow these steps in a collision where there are no injuries:

1. If the vehicles are driveable, move them as far off the road as possible — this should not affect the police officer's investigation. This is especially important on busy or high speed roads where it may be dangerous to leave vehicles in the driving lanes. If you cannot move the vehicles off the road, set up warning signals or flares far enough away to give other traffic time to slow down or stop.

2. Call police (provincial or local, depending on where the collision takes place). By law, you must report any collision to the police where there are injuries or damage to vehicles or property exceeding $1,000.

3. Give all possible help to police or anyone whose vehicle has been damaged. This includes giving police your name and address, the name and address of the registered owner of the vehicle, the vehicle plate and permit number and the liability insurance card.

4. Get the names, addresses and phone numbers of all witnesses.

5. If damage is less than $1,000, you are still required by law to exchange information with anyone whose vehicle has been damaged. However, the collision does not have to be reported to the police.

6. Contact your insurance company as soon as possible if you intend to make a claim.

TRAFFIC SIGNS AND LIGHTS

Traffic laws include the traffic signs and lights, pedestrian signals and pavement markings that tell drivers and other road users what they must do in certain situations. This chapter shows you what many of those signs, lights and markings look like and explains what they mean to drivers.

I. Signs

Traffic signs give you important information about the law, warn you about dangerous conditions and help you find your way. Signs use different symbols, colours and shapes for easy identification.

Here are some of the many signs you will see on Ontario roads:

A stop sign is eight-sided and has a red background with white letters. It means you must come to a complete stop. Stop at the stop line if it is marked on the pavement. If there is no stop line, stop at the crosswalk, marked or not. If there is no crosswalk, stop at the edge of the sidewalk. If there is no sidewalk, stop at the edge of the intersection. Wait until the way is clear before entering the intersection.

A school zone sign is five-sided and has a blue background with white symbols. It warns that you are coming to a school zone. Slow down, drive with extra caution, and watch for children.

I. Signs

A yield sign is a triangle with a white background and a red border. It means you must let traffic in the intersection or close to it go first. Stop if necessary and go only when the way is clear.

A railway crossing sign is X-shaped with a white background and red outline. It warns that railway tracks cross the road. Watch for this sign. Slow down and look both ways for trains. Be prepared to stop.

There are four other kinds of signs: regulatory, warning, temporary conditions, and information and direction.

Regulatory signs

These signs give a direction that must be obeyed. They are usually rectangular or square with a white or black background and black, white or coloured letters.

A sign with a green circle means you may or must do the activity shown inside the ring. A red circle with a line through it means the activity shown is not allowed.

Here are some common regulatory signs:

This road is an official bicycle route. Watch for cyclists and be prepared to share the road with them.

You may park in the area between the signs during the times posted. (Used in pairs or groups.)

Snowmobiles may use this road.

Do not enter this road.

Do not stop in the area between the signs. This means you may not stop your vehicle in this area, even for a moment. (Used in pairs or groups.)

Do not stand in the area between the signs. This means you may not stop your vehicle in this area except to load or unload passengers or merchandise. (Used in pairs or groups.)

Do not park in the area between the signs. This means you may not stop your vehicle except to load or unload passengers or merchandise. (Used in pairs or groups.)

Do not turn left at the intersection.

Do not drive through the intersection.

Do not turn to go in the opposite direction. (U-turn)

Do not turn right when facing a red light at the intersection.

Do not turn left during the times shown.

This parking space is only for vehicles displaying a valid Disabled Person Parking Permit.

No bicycles allowed on this road.

63

I. Signs

 No pedestrians allowed on this road.

 Slow traffic on multi-lane roads must keep right.

   These signs, above the road or on the pavement before an intersection, tell drivers the direction they must travel. For example: the driver in lane one must turn left; the driver in lane two must turn left or go straight ahead; and the driver in lane three must turn right.

 Keep to the right of the traffic island.

 Speed limit changes ahead.

 The speed limit in this zone is lower during school hours. Observe the speed limit shown when the yellow lights are flashing.

 Traffic may travel in one direction only.

  This is a pedestrian crossing or crossover. You must yield the right-of-way to pedestrians.

 Do not pass on this road.

This sign, above the road or on the ground, means the lane is only for two-way left turns.

These signs mean lanes are only for specific types of vehicles, either all the time or during certain hours. Different symbols are used for the different types of vehicles. They include: buses, taxis, vehicles with three or more people, and bicycles.

Keep to the right lane except when passing on two-lane sections where climbing lanes are provided.

This sign reserves curb area for picking up and dropping off passengers with disabilities.

65

I. Signs

Warning signs

These signs warn of dangerous or unusual conditions ahead such as a curve, turn, dip or sideroad. They are usually diamond-shaped and have a yellow background with black letters or symbols.

Here are some common warning signs:

Intersection ahead. The arrow shows which direction of traffic has the right-of-way.

Drivers on the sideroad at the intersection ahead don't have a clear view of traffic.

Posted under a curve warning, this sign shows the maximum safe speed for the curve.

Sharp bend or turn in the road ahead.

Narrow bridge ahead.

Pavement narrows ahead.

Chevron (arrowhead) signs are posted in groups to guide drivers around sharp curves in the road.

Road branching off ahead.

Slight bend or curve in the road ahead.

Winding road ahead.

The bridge ahead lifts or swings to let boats pass.

 Paved surface ends ahead.

 Bicycle crossing ahead.

 Stop sign ahead. Slow down.

 Share the road with oncoming traffic.

 Pavement is slippery when wet. Slow down and drive with caution.

 Hazard close to the edge of the road. The downward lines show the side on which you may safely pass.

 The road ahead is split into two separate roads by a median. Keep to the right-hand road. Each road carries one-way traffic.

 Right lane ends ahead. If you are in the right-hand lane you must merge safely with traffic in the lane to the left.

I. Signs

 Traffic lights ahead. Slow down.

 Snowmobiles cross this road.

 Bump or uneven pavement on the road ahead. Slow down and keep control of your vehicle.

 Steep hill ahead. You may need to use a lower gear.

 Traffic travels in both directions on the same road ahead. Keep to the right.

 Railway crossing ahead. Be alert for trains. This sign also shows the angle at which the railway tracks cross the road.

 Two roads going in the same direction are about to join into one. Drivers on both are equally responsible for seeing that traffic merges smoothly and safely.

 Underpass ahead. Take care if you are driving a tall vehicle. Sign shows how much room you have.

 Sharp turn or bend in the road in the direction of the arrow. The checkerboard border warns of danger. Slow down; be careful.

Deer regularly cross this road; be alert for animals.

 Watch for pedestrians and be prepared to share the road with them.

 This sign warns you that you are coming to a hidden school bus stop. Slow down, drive with extra caution, watch for children and for a school bus with flashing red lights.

 Truck entrance on the right side of the road ahead. If the sign shows the truck on the left, the entrance is on the left side of the road.

 Watch for fallen rock and be prepared to avoid a collision.

  These signs warn of a school crossing. Watch for children and follow the directions of the crossing guard or school safety patroller.

 Shows maximum safe speed on ramp.

 There may be water flowing over the road.

I. Signs

Temporary condition signs

These signs warn of unusual temporary conditions such as road work zones, diversions, detours, lane closures or traffic control people on the road. They are usually diamond-shaped with an orange background and black letters or symbols.

Here are some common temporary condition signs:

Survey crew working on the road ahead.

Temporary detour from normal traffic route.

Traffic control person ahead. Drive slowly and watch for instructions.

Flashing lights on the arrows show the direction to follow.

Construction work one kilometre ahead.

You are entering a construction zone. Drive with extra caution and be prepared for a lower speed limit.

Road work ahead.

Pavement has been milled or grooved. Your vehicle's stopping ability may be affected so obey the speed limit and drive with extra caution. Motorcyclists may experience reduced traction on these surfaces.

Lane ahead is closed for road-work. Obey the speed limit and merge with traffic in the open lane.

Closed lane. Adjust speed to merge with traffic in lane indicated by arrow.

Do not pass the pilot or pace vehicle bearing this sign.

Reduce speed and be prepared to stop.

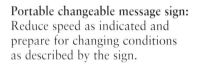

Portable changeable message sign: Reduce speed as indicated and prepare for changing conditions as described by the sign.

I. Signs

Information and direction signs

These signs tell you about distances and destinations. They are usually rectangular with a green background and white letters. Other signs with different colours guide you to facilities, services and attractions.

Here are some common information and direction signs:

 Shows directions to nearby towns and cities.

 Shows the distances in kilometres to towns and cities on the road.

 Various exit signs are used on freeways.

In urban areas, many exit ramps have more than one lane. Overhead and ground-mounted signs help drivers choose the correct lane to exit or stay on the freeway.

 Advance signs use arrows to show which lanes lead off the freeway. Signs are also posted at the exit.

Emergency response signs

 Some information signs include a numbering system along the bottom of the sign to assist emergency vehicles in determining an appropriate route.

 Sometimes one or more lanes may lead off the freeway. The arrows matching the exit lanes are shown on the advance sign in a yellow box with the word 'exit' under them.

 Freeway interchanges or exits have numbers that correspond to the distance from the beginning of the freeway. For example, interchange number 203 on Highway 401 is 203 kilometres from Windsor, where the freeway begins. Distances can be calculated by subtracting one interchange number from another.

 The term 'VIA' is used to describe the roads that must be followed to reach a destination.

These signs change according to traffic conditions to give drivers current information on delays and lane closures ahead.

 Shows route to passenger railway station.

 Shows route to airport.

 Shows route to ferry service.

Shows facilities available such as fuel, food, accommodation or camping.

 Shows types of fuel available:
D — diesel;
P — propane;
N — natural gas.

 Shows facilities that are accessible by wheelchair.

I. Signs

STOP FOR
SCHOOL BUS
WHEN SIGNALS
FLASHING

Stop for school
bus when signals
are flashing.

No trucks over 6.5 m
in indicated lane.

Road forks
to the right.

No trucks in
this lane.

No trucks over
6.5 m in this lane.

No heavy trucks
permitted on this
roadway.

No trucks in
indicated lane.

Heavy trucks
permitted on
this roadway.

No heavy trucks
permitted on this
roadway between the
hours of 7pm - 7am.

MAXIMUM WEIGHT 10 tonnes

No vehicles over 10 tonnes on this roadway.

CLASS B ROAD

Class B roadway.

Trucks carrying dangerous materials are not permitted on this roadway.

LOAD RESTRICTION IN EFFECT 5 tonnes per axle

No vehicles that bear more than 5 tonnes per axle permitted on this roadway.

DANGEROUS GOODS ROUTE

Trucks carrying dangerous materials permitted on this roadway.

DANGEROUS GOODS CARRIERS PROHIBITED

No vehicles containing hazardous materials permitted on this roadway.

MAXIMUM WEIGHT 00 00 00 tonnes

Indicates different weight restrictions for different types of heavy trucks for a bridge structure.

Trucks carrying dangerous materials permitted on this roadway.

SCHOOL BUS LOADING ZONE →

School bus loading zone, proceed with caution.

I. Signs

TRUCKS ENTER INSPECTION STATION
WHEN LIGHTS FLASHING

Trucks must enter inspection station when signals are flashing.

407 ETR
Express Toll Route
Vehicles Over 5 Tonnes Must Have Valid Transponder

Any trucks over 5 tonnes must have a valid 407 transponder to use ETR.

USE LOWER GEAR

Trucks are advised to use a lower gear when travelling this portion of roadway.

ONE LANE ONLY WHEN USED BY TRUCKS

Indicates that horizontal clearance does not allow room for another vehicle when structure is being used by a truck.

Maximum vertical clearance of 3.9 m.

Maximum vertical-clearance of 3.9 m under this obstruction.

Indicates that an upcoming structure might not allow room for a tall truck, and should therefore choose an alternate route.

WHEN FLASHING

Tab indicates that sign has pertinence when lights are flashing.

Trucks are advised to slow down around this curve due to it's smaller radius.

MAXIMUM 10 tonnes

Trucks over 10 tonnes are advised not to use this roadway.

TRUCK ENTRANCE

Indicates an upcoming truck entrance and vehicles should be prepared to yield to Trucks entering the roadway.

FIRE TRUCK ENTRANCE

Indicates an upcoming fire truck entrance and vehicles should be prepared to yield to trucks entering the roadway.

MAXIMUM 00 00 00 tonnes

Advises trucks to use caution if they are over indicated weight restrictions for their truck type.

Indicates an upcoming bus entrance on the right and vehicles should be prepared to yield to trucks entering the roadway.

SCHOOL BUS STOP AHEAD

School bus stop ahead, proceed with caution.

Indicates an upcoming truck entrance on the right and vehicles should be prepared to yield to trucks entering the roadway.

Indicates an upcoming fire truck entrance on the right and vehicles should be prepared to yield to trucks entering the roadway.

I. Signs

Other signs

Here are some other common signs:

The slow-moving vehicle sign is orange with a red border. Motor vehicles moving slower than 40 km/h must show this sign at the rear when driving on a road, unless they are only crossing it.

The new driver sign has a green background with black lettering. Placed in the back window of a vehicle, it tells other drivers that the driver is a novice.

Bilingual signs

Watch for these signs when driving in designated bilingual areas. Read the messages in the language you understand best. Bilingual messages may be together on the same sign or separate, with an English sign immediately followed by a French sign.

II. Traffic lights

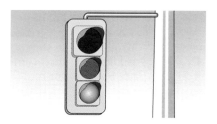  

Traffic lights guide drivers and pedestrians through intersections and along roads. They tell road users when to stop and go, when and how to turn and when to drive with extra caution.

Green light

A green light means you may turn left, go straight or turn right after yielding to vehicles and pedestrians already in the intersection. When turning left or right you must yield the right-of-way to pedestrians crossing the intersection.

Yellow light

A yellow — or amber — light means the red light is about to appear. You must stop if you can do so safely; otherwise, go with caution.

Red light

A red light means you must stop. Bring your vehicle to a complete stop at the stop line if it is marked on the pavement. If there is no stop line, stop at the crosswalk, marked or not. If there is no crosswalk, stop at the edge of the sidewalk. If there is no sidewalk, stop at the edge of the intersection.

II. Traffic lights

Wait until the light changes to green and the intersection is clear before moving through it.

Unless a sign tells you not to, you may turn right on a red light only after coming to a complete stop and waiting until the way is clear. You may also turn left on a red light if you are moving from a one-way road into a one-way road, but you must come to a complete stop first and wait until the way is clear.

Lights and arrows to help turning vehicles

Flashing green lights and green arrows direct drivers who are turning.

Advance green light or arrow

When you face a flashing green light or a left-pointing green arrow and a green light, you may turn left, go straight ahead or turn right from the proper lane. This is called an advanced green light because oncoming traffic still faces a red light.

Pedestrians must not cross on a flashing green light unless a pedestrian signal tells them to.

Simultaneous left turn

When a left-turn green arrow is shown with a red light, you may turn left from the left-turn lane. Vehicles turning left from the opposite direction may also be making left turns because they too face a left-turn green arrow.

After the left-turn green arrow, a yellow arrow may appear. This means the green light is about to appear for traffic in both directions. Do not start your left turn. Stop if you can do so safely; otherwise, complete your turn with caution.

You can still turn left when the light is green, but only when the way is clear of traffic and pedestrians. If the light turns red when you are in the intersection, complete your turn when it is safe.

Pedestrians must not cross on a left-turn green arrow unless a pedestrian signal tells them to.

Transit priority signals

Traffic and pedestrians must yield to public transit vehicles at a transit priority signal. The round signal is on top of a regular traffic signal and shows a white vertical bar on a dark background. This allows transit vehicles to go through, turn right or left, while all conflicting traffic faces a red light.

II. Traffic lights

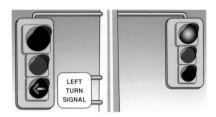

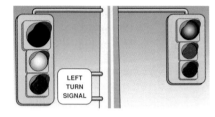

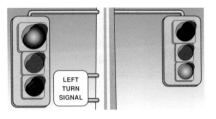

Fully protected left turn

Some intersections have separate traffic lights for left-turning traffic and for traffic going through the intersection or turning right.

When a left-turn green arrow appears for traffic in the left-turn lane, traffic going straight ahead or turning right will usually see a red light. You may turn left from the left-turn lane when you face a green arrow. Vehicles from the opposite direction may also be turning left.

After the left-turn green arrow, a yellow light appears for left-turning vehicles only.

After the yellow light, a red light appears for left-turning vehicles only. Traffic going straight ahead or turning right will face a green light or green arrows pointing straight ahead and to the right.

In these intersections, you may not begin turning left after the green light appears for traffic going straight ahead or turning right. If the light turns yellow while you are in the intersection, complete your turn with caution.

II. Traffic lights

Flashing red light
You must come to a complete stop at a flashing red light. Move through the intersection only when it is safe.

Flashing yellow light
A flashing yellow light means you should drive with caution when approaching and moving through the intersection.

Blank traffic lights
During an electrical power loss, traffic lights at intersections will not work. Yield the right-of-way to vehicles in the intersection and to vehicles entering the intersection from your right.

Go cautiously and use the intersection the same way you would use an intersection with all-way stop signs.

Traffic beacons
A traffic beacon is a single flashing light hung over an intersection or placed over signs or on obstacles in the road.

Flashing red beacon
A flashing red beacon above an intersection or stop sign means you must come to a complete stop. Move through the intersection only when it is safe to do so.

Flashing yellow beacon
A flashing yellow beacon above an intersection, above a warning sign or on an obstruction in the road, warns you to drive with caution.

III. Pedestrian signals

Pedestrian signals help pedestrians cross at intersections with traffic lights. The signal for pedestrians to walk is a white walking symbol. A flashing or steady orange hand symbol means pedestrians must not begin to cross.

A pedestrian facing a walk signal may cross the road in the direction of the signal. While crossing, pedestrians have the right-of-way over all vehicles.

Where there are pedestrian pushbuttons, a pedestrian must use the button to bring on the walk signal. Pedestrian signals give people more time to cross than regular traffic lights.

A pedestrian facing a flashing or steady hand symbol should not begin to cross the road. Pedestrians who have already begun to cross when the hand signal appears, should go as quickly as possible to a safe area. While they are crossing, pedestrians still have the right-of-way over vehicles.

At intersections with traffic lights where there are no pedestrian signals, pedestrians facing a green light may cross. Pedestrians may not cross on a flashing green light or a left-turn green arrow.

Intersection pedestrian signals

On a busy main road, an intersection pedestrian signal helps people to cross the road safely by signalling traffic to stop. The intersection

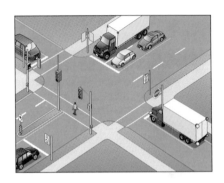

pedestrian signal has one or more crosswalks, pedestrian walk and don't walk signals, push buttons for pedestrians, and traffic signal lights on the main road only. Stop signs control traffic on the smaller, less busy crossroad.

You must observe, obey the traffic rules, and use your safe driving skills to drive through these intersections. (See Yielding the right-of way on page 31.)

IV. Pavement markings

Pavement markings work with road signs and traffic lights to give you important information about the direction of traffic and where you may and may not travel. Pavement markings divide traffic lanes, show turning lanes, mark pedestrian crossings, indicate obstacles, and tell you when it is not safe to pass.

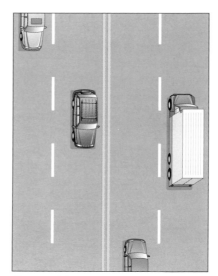

Diagram 4-1

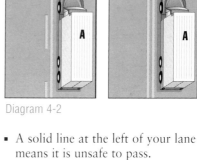

Diagram 4-2

- Yellow lines separate traffic travelling in opposite directions. White lines separate traffic travelling in the same direction.

- A solid line at the left of your lane means it is unsafe to pass. ('A' should not pass.)

IV. Pavement markings

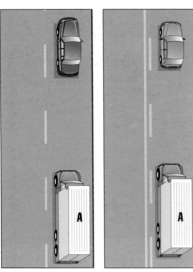

Diagram 4-3

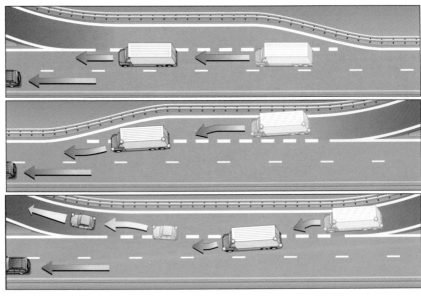

- A broken line at the left of your lane means you may pass if the way is clear. ('A' may pass if there are enough broken lines ahead to complete the pass safely.)

- Broken lines that are wider and closer together than regular broken lines are called continuity lines. When you see continuity lines on your left side, it means the lane you are in is ending or exiting and that you must change lanes if you want to continue in your current direction. Continuity lines on your right mean your lane will continue unaffected **(Diagram 4-4: Above)**.

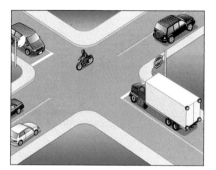

Diagram 4-5

Diagram 4-6

Diagram 4-7

- A stop line is a single white line painted across the road at an intersection. It shows where you must stop. If there is no stop line marked on the road, stop at the crosswalk, marked or not. If there is no crosswalk, stop at the edge of the sidewalk. If there is no sidewalk, stop at the edge of the intersection.

- A crosswalk is marked by two parallel white lines painted across the road. However, crosswalks at intersections are not always marked. If there is no stop line, stop at the crosswalk, marked or not. If there is no crosswalk, stop at the edge of the sidewalk. If there is no sidewalk, stop at the edge of the intersection.

- A white arrow painted on a lane means you may move only in the direction of the arrow.

IV. Pavement markings

Diagram 4-8

Diagram 4-9

- A pedestrian crossing — or crossover — is marked by two white double parallel lines across the road with an X in each lane approaching it. Stop before the line and yield to pedestrians.

- Two solid lines painted on the pavement guide traffic away from fixed objects such as bridge piers or concrete islands. Yellow and black markings are also painted on the objects themselves as warnings.

KEEPING YOUR LICENCE

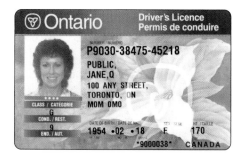

I. Keeping your licence

Ontario has a one-piece plastic driver's licence. The licence card has a digitized photograph and signature of the driver and a magnetic information stripe. All drivers in Ontario should have a one-piece licence card.

You must carry your licence with you whenever you drive.

I. Keeping your licence

Renewing your licence

When your licence is due for renewal, you will get a renewal application form in the mail. Most drivers are required to a pass a vision and a written test at time of renewal. **If any tests are required, you must renew your licence at a Driver Examination Centre.** However, if tests are not required, you may renew your licence in person at any Driver and Vehicle Licence Office, or by mail, following the instructions on the renewal application.

If you do not get a renewal application form in the mail when your licence is due for renewal, call the Ministry of Transportation. You are responsible for making sure you have a valid driver's licence. You can renew an expired bus or truck driver's licence within one year without taking a road test.

If your licence has been suspended, cancelled or expired for more than three years, you will be required to reapply for a licence in Ontario and meet all the requirements of graduated licensing including passing all the required tests.

If you have any commercial vehicle driver's licence other than a class 'D' licence, you must pass a medical examination every three years. You will get a notice in the mail three months before your medical report is due. You must go to a doctor and get a medical examination. The doctor will complete the form that you must submit to the Ministry of Transportation, either by mail or in person. If you do not file a medical report, your class of licence will be downgraded.

Commercial vehicle drivers aged 65 and older must pass a vision, written and road test every year. For drivers with a class 'D' licence, annual vision, written and road tests are necessary at 80 years of age and older.

Changing your name or address

You must tell the Ministry of Transportation within six days of changing your name or address.

You will need a new licence when you change your address. Take the change of information form to a Driver and Vehicle Licence Office, or mail it to the Ministry of Transportation, P.O. Box 9200, Kingston, ON, K7L 5K4. The ministry will send you a new licence. When you get it, destroy your old licence and carry the new one with you whenever you drive.

If you change your name, you need a new licence. Take the documents you must show (see the chart below) and your current licence to a Driver and Vehicle Licence Office. A new photograph will be taken. You will get a temporary licence to use until your permanent licence is mailed to you. Carry it with you whenever you drive.

There is no charge for getting a new licence because you change your name or address.

The chart on this page shows the documents you will need to change your name on your driver's licence. If you don't have the proper documents, the ministry will look at your case individually.

REASON FOR NAME CHANGE	DOCUMENTATION REQUIRED
Marriage	Marriage certificate
Common-law alliance	Notarized affidavit of the fact
Adoption	Adoption papers
Under the Change of Name Act	Change of name certificate

II. The demerit point system

Driver's licence laws

It is illegal to lend your licence or let someone else use it. It is also illegal to have an altered licence, to use another licence as your own, or to have more than one Ontario driver's licence.

The demerit point system encourages drivers to improve their behaviour and protects people from drivers who abuse the privilege of driving. Drivers convicted of driving-related offences have demerit points recorded on their records. (See the point system table on page 93.) Demerit points stay on your record for two years from the date of the offence. If you get enough demerit points, you can lose your driver's licence.

If you get six demerit points, you will be told about your record and urged to improve your driving habits.

At nine points, you may have to go to an interview to discuss your record and give reasons why your licence should not be suspended.

You may also have to complete a driver re-examination. If you fail this test, your licence can be cancelled. If you fail to attend an interview, or fail to give good reasons for keeping your licence, your licence may be suspended.

At 15 points, your licence will be suspended for 30 days from the date you hand over your licence to a Driver and Vehicle Licence Office. You can lose your licence for up to two years if you fail to hand over your licence.

After the suspension, the number of points on your driver's record will be reduced to seven. Any extra points could again bring you to the interview level. If you reach 15 points again, your licence will be suspended for six months.

TABLE OF OFFENCES

Here are the demerit point penalties for driving offences.

7 points

- Failing to remain at the scene of a collision
- Failing to stop for police

6 points

- Careless driving
- Racing
- Exceeding the speed limit by 50 km/h or more
- Failing to stop for a school bus

5 points

- Driver of bus failing to stop at unprotected railway crossing

4 points

- Exceeding the speed limit by 30 to 49 km/h
- Following too closely

3 points

- Exceeding the speed limit by 16 to 29 km/h
- Driving through, around or under a railway crossing barrier
- Failing to yield the right-of-way
- Failing to obey a stop sign, traffic light or railway crossing signal
- Failing to obey the directions of a police officer
- Driving the wrong way on a divided road
- Failing to report a collision to a police officer
- Improper driving where road is divided into lanes
- Crowding the driver's seat
- Going the wrong way on a one-way road
- Driving or operating a vehicle on a closed road
- Crossing a divided road where no proper crossing is provided

2 points

- Failing to lower headlight beam
- Improper opening of a vehicle door
- Prohibited turns
- Towing people — on toboggans, bicycles, skis, for example
- Failing to obey signs
- Failing to stop at a pedestrian crossing
- Failing to share the road
- Improper right turn
- Improper left turn
- Failing to signal
- Unnecessary slow driving
- Reversing on a divided high-speed road
- Driver failing to wear a seat belt
- Driver failing to ensure that a passenger less than 23 kg is buckled into seat belt or child safety seat
- Driver failing to ensure passenger under 16 years wearing seat belt

III. Other ways to lose your licence

You may also lose your licence for the following reasons:

Medical suspension

By law, all doctors must report the names and addresses of everyone 16 years or older who has a condition that may affect their ability to drive safely. Addiction to alcohol or drugs are conditions that affect your ability to drive. Doctors report this information to the Ministry of Transportation and it is not given to anyone else. Your driver's licence may be suspended until new medical evidence shows that the condition does not pose a safety risk.

Discretionary HTA suspensions

Your licence **may** be suspended:
- If you don't tell the truth:
  - in an application, declaration, affidavit or paper required by the Highway Traffic Act, its Regulations or the Ministry of Transportation.
  - about vehicle liability insurance.
- If you fail to insure your vehicle.
- If you are convicted of some driving offenses, including careless driving and driving 50 km/h or more over the speed limit.

Mandatory HTA suspensions

Your licence **will** be suspended:
- If you are convicted of failing to stop for a police officer and the court believes you willfully avoided police during pursuit — that you tried to escape the police. (Your licence will be suspended for a minimum of five years.)
- If you don't pay a traffic fine when ordered by the court.

Administrative suspension

Your licence will be suspended **immediately** for 90 days:

- If you fail or refuse to give a breath or blood sample when asked by the police.
- If your blood alcohol concentration is more than 80 milligrams in 100 millilitres of blood (.08).

This suspension takes effect while you are still at the roadside or at the police station. It is an administrative suspension by the Registrar of Motor Vehicles and is separate from any criminal charges or prosecution that may also take place.

Your licence will be cancelled:

- If you fail a driver's re-examination.
- If you don't pay your reinstatement fee.
- If your cheque for licence fees is not honoured by your bank.
- If you voluntarily surrender your driver's licence to the Ministry of Transportation or it is surrendered or returned by another jurisdiction.

Criminal Code suspensions

You will receive a one-year licence suspension the first time you are convicted of a Criminal Code offence. If you are convicted of a second Criminal Code offence, your licence will be suspended for three years. A third Criminal Code offence will get you a lifetime suspension from driving with the possibility of reinstatement after 10 years. Fourth time offenders convicted of a Criminal Code offence are suspended from driving for life with no possibility of reinstatement. Convictions will remain on your driver's record for a minimum of 10 years. The court may order that the mandatory period of a suspension for a Criminal Code offence be extended.

III. Other ways to lose your licence

Your licence will be suspended if you are convicted of any of the following Criminal Code offences:

- Driving or having care and control of a vehicle while your ability is impaired by alcohol or drugs
- Refusing to submit to a breath test for alcohol
- Failing or refusing to provide a breath sample for roadside testing
- Driving or having care and control of a vehicle when your blood alcohol concentration is more than 80 milligrams in 100 millilitres of blood (.08)
- Failing to remain at the scene of a collision to escape criminal or civil liability
- Dangerous driving
- Causing bodily harm by criminal negligence
- Causing death by criminal negligence

Remedial measures

If you are convicted of a driving-related Criminal Code offence, you must complete a remedial program before you can get your licence back. There are two types of remedial programs:

- If you are convicted of a drinking and driving related Criminal Code offence, you must take the impaired driving program called Back on Track, delivered by the Centre of Addiction and Mental Health. The three-part program, which is available across the province, involves assessment, education or treatment and follow-up. You must pay the cost of the program directly to the program provider.
- If you are convicted of a non-drinking and driving related Criminal Code offence and have no previous alcohol related convictions, you must undergo a Ministry of Transportation driver improvement interview.

If you have not completed your remedial program by the time your Criminal Code suspension expires, your licence will be further suspended until you have completed the remedial requirements.

Reinstatement fees

Suspended drivers must pay $100 to have their licence reinstated. This fee does not apply to reinstatement following a medical or administrative suspension of your driver's licence.

Driving under suspension

You may not drive, under any circumstances, when your licence is suspended. If you are convicted of driving while your licence is suspended for an HTA offence, you will have to pay a fine of $1,000 to $5,000 for a first offence and $2,000 to $5,000 for a 'subsequent' offence. (A 'subsequent' offence is when you are convicted again within five years.) You may have to spend six months in jail, or you may have to pay a fine or do both. Your licence will be suspended for an additional six months.

There is a fine for driving when your licence is cancelled.

If you are found guilty of driving while your licence is suspended for a Criminal Code offence, you face a fine of $5,000 to $25,000 for a first offence and $10,000 to $50,000 for a subsequent offence within five years. You also face an additional suspension (one year for a first offence; two years for a subsequent offence) under the HTA, and up to two years in prison and three years licence suspension under the Criminal Code.

Driving While Prohibited

This is a prohibition order under the Criminal Code Conviction. When convicted of violation of order, you will get a suspension of one year for a first offence or two years for a subsequent offence. Courts can order longer prohibition, which will be matched in length by a suspension under the Highway Traffic Act.

III. Other ways to lose your licence

Vehicle Impoundment Program

If you are caught driving while your licence is suspended for a Criminal Code offence, the vehicle you are driving will be impounded. This applies whether the vehicle is borrowed from a friend or family member, used for business or employment purposes, rented or leased. The vehicle will be placed in an impound yard for a minimum of 45 days. The owner of the vehicle must pay the towing and storage costs before the vehicle will be released. This program applies to all motor vehicles including passenger vehicles, motorcycles, trucks and buses.

The Vehicle Impoundment Program makes vehicle owners responsible for ensuring that anyone driving their vehicles is not suspended for a Criminal Code conviction. People loaning or renting their vehicles can verify that a driver's licence is valid by phone at 1-900-565-6555 or online at www.mto.gov.on.ca/english/dandv/catalogue.htm. You can also get a driver's abstract at Driver and Vehicle Licence Offices or Service Ontario Kiosks. There is a nominal fee for each licence checked.

Impaired driving

Impaired driving, which means driving when your ability is affected by alcohol or drugs, is a crime in Canada. Your vehicle does not even have to be moving; you can be charged if you are impaired behind the wheel, even if you have not started to drive.

Alcohol

Drinking and driving is a deadly combination.

All drivers must be able to concentrate on driving. Even one drink can reduce your ability to concentrate, to watch out for and react to things that happen suddenly when you are driving. With more alcohol in your blood, you could have trouble judging distances and your vision may become blurred. Factors like fatigue, your mood and how long ago you ate and how much, can make a difference in how alcohol affects your driving ability.

The police have the right to stop any driver they suspect is impaired. They may also do roadside spot checks. When you are stopped by the police, you may be told to blow into a machine that tests your breath for alcohol — a roadside screening device. If you refuse, you will be charged under the Criminal Code. The police will also notify the

Registrar of Motor Vehicles and your licence will be suspended immediately for 90 days.

If the reading on the machine shows you have been drinking, you may be taken to a police station for a breathalyser test. The breathalyser uses your breath to measure the amount of alcohol in your bloodstream.

If you cannot give a breath sample for some reason, the police officer can ask you to let a doctor take a blood sample instead. If you are injured and cannot give your consent, a justice of the peace may authorize a doctor to take a blood sample.

The maximum legal blood alcohol concentration for fully licensed drivers is 80 milligrams in 100 millilitres of blood (.08). Any more than .08 is against the law.

If your reading is less than .08 but .05 or more, or if you register 'warn' on a roadside screening device, the police can suspend your licence for 12 hours. This keeps you from driving

until your blood alcohol level drops. You must give your licence to the police officer on demand. The police will tell you when the 12-hour suspension will end and where to get your licence back. Meanwhile, if there is no one else available to drive and no safe place to park your vehicle, it will be towed at your expense.

If your blood alcohol concentration is more than 80 milligrams in 100 millilitres of blood (.08), you will be charged under the Criminal Code. The police will also notify the Registrar of Motor Vehicles and your licence will be suspended immediately for 90 days. Even if your blood alcohol concentration is less than .08, you can still be charged with impaired driving under the Criminal Code.

III. Other ways to lose your licence

Drugs

Any drug that changes your mood or the way you see and feel about the world around you will affect the way you drive. The Criminal Code and HTA suspensions apply to drivers impaired by alcohol or drugs.

Illegal drugs such as marijuana and cocaine are not the only problem. Some drugs that your doctor may prescribe for you and some over-the-counter drugs can also impair your driving. Here are some points you should remember:

- If you use prescription medicines or get allergy shots, ask your doctor about side effects such as dizziness, blurred vision, nausea or drowsiness that could affect your driving.
- Read the information on the package of any over-the-counter medicine you take. Any stimulant, diet pill, tranquillizer or sedative may affect your driving. Even allergy and cold remedies may have ingredients that could affect your driving.

- Drugs and alcohol together can have dangerous effects, even several days after you have taken the drug. Do not take a chance — ask your doctor or pharmacist.

Consider the consequences

Having your licence suspended is not the only cost of impaired driving. Depending on whether it is your first, second, third or fourth offence, you can be fined, sent to jail for up to five years and prohibited from driving for the rest of your life.

For impaired driving that causes injury or death, the penalties are even more severe. If you are convicted of impaired driving causing bodily harm, you may be sentenced to up to 10 years in prison. Impaired driving causing death can carry a sentence of up to 14 years in prison.

If you have been drinking and driving and are involved in a collision, your insurance company may not have to pay for damage to your vehicle. If you are injured in the collision, your medical and rehabilitation costs may not be covered.

If you drive for a living, a licence suspension could mean losing your job. And when you do get your licence back, you may find your insurance costs 50 to 100 per cent more for at least three years.

ADDITIONAL INFORMATION

Over the past years, it has become obvious that there is a need for truck drivers to keep up to date on legislation, regulation and policy concerning truck transportation. That is why the Ministry of Transportation offers CMV News on the World-Wide Web; visit http://www.mto.gov.on.ca/english/safety/cmv/.

I. Ontario's Drive Clean program

Vehicles powered by gasoline and diesel give off air pollutants and gases such as oxides of carbon, nitrogen and sulphur, hydrocarbons and soot. These pollutants affect the quality of the air we breathe, our health, crop yields and even the global climate.

Hydrocarbons and oxides of nitrogen react in sunlight to form ground level ozone, better known as smog. Smog is a major health hazard responsible for respiratory ailments and other illnesses.

Oxides of sulphur and nitrogen combine with water vapour to form acid rain, which damages our lakes, forests and crops.

Global warming is the result of too much carbon dioxide and other gases trapping heat in our atmosphere. Global warming could cause average temperatures to rise, causing droughts, crop failures, lower water levels and more frequent and severe storms.

Ontario's Drive Clean program is designed to reduce smog-causing emissions from vehicles. Vehicles are responsible for a substantial amount of the pollutants in and around our urban areas, but Drive Clean testing of vehicle emissions can help make a difference in the quality of air we breathe.

If you own a light-duty vehicle that is between three and 20 years older than its model year, you must take your vehicle for a Drive Clean test every two years in order to renew its registration. If you are buying a used vehicle that is older than the current model year, the vehicle must be tested to transfer the ownership and put licence plates on it.

Ontario requires all diesel-powered heavy-duty trucks and buses province-wide to pass an annual Drive Clean emissions test. All non-diesel heavy-duty vehicles require annual tests if they are registered in the designated Drive Clean light-duty vehicle program area.

For more information on Ontario's Drive Clean program, visit www.driveclean.com or call the Drive Clean Call Centre toll-free at 1-888-758-2999.